Wish I Knew That Sooner

Wish I Knew That Sooner

STRATEGIES TO AVOID
FINANCIAL REGRET

STEN MORGAN CFP®

Advantage®

Published by Advantage, Charleston, South Carolina.
Member of Advantage Media Group.

ADVANTAGE is a registered trademark, and the Advantage colophon is a trademark of Advantage Media Group, Inc.

Printed in the United States of America.

10 9 8 7 6 5 4 3 2 1

ISBN: 978-1-64225-300-9
LCCN: 2020925527

Cover design by Megan Elger.
Layout design by Carly Blake.

This publication is designed to provide accurate and authoritative information in regard to the subject matter covered. It is sold with the understanding that the publisher is not engaged in rendering legal, accounting, or other professional services. If legal advice or other expert assistance is required, the services of a competent professional person should be sought.

Advantage Media Group is proud to be a part of the Tree Neutral® program. Tree Neutral offsets the number of trees consumed in the production and printing of this book by taking proactive steps such as planting trees in direct proportion to the number of trees used to print books. To learn more about Tree Neutral, please visit **www.treeneutral.com**.

Advantage Media Group is a publisher of business, self-improvement, and professional development books and online learning. We help entrepreneurs, business leaders, and professionals share their Stories, Passion, and Knowledge to help others Learn & Grow. Do you have a manuscript or book idea that you would like us to consider for publishing? Please visit **advantagefamily.com** or call **1.843.414.5600**.

To Taylor, Scarlett, Layla, and Jacoby. You motivate me every day to be better and love me even when I am not.

Heavenly Father, thank you for always being present, carrying me through hard times, and teaching me what is most important.

Contents

Introduction

Ron Wayne probably wishes he had known sooner. Wayne is the little-known "third cofounder" of Apple, joining Steve Jobs and Steve Wozniak in the company's inception in the mid-1970s. Jobs and Wozniak were young (and broke) tech whizzes, and Wayne agreed to lend a hand with his personal assets and engineering assistance in exchange for 10% ownership. Everything appeared great on the outset, but Wayne feared future financial responsibility if the start-up company fizzled out. He took his name off the contract after just twelve days and sold his shares back to his partners for $800. As I write this book, Apple has reached a new all-time high and is worth around $2 trillion. So, a 10% stake today would be close to $200 billion.

Wayne's story is a case of foresight versus hindsight. It's always easy to say what you should have done after the fact. After all, hindsight is 20/20. Foresight, however, makes all the difference. Had Wayne known his stake in an upstart little company would turn into billions, he likely would have made different decisions and led a markedly different life. Unfortunately, he didn't have that knowledge and instead ended up with a big regret.

Wayne's story can teach us a lot about money: foresight is better than hindsight. Some people will tell you time is the most powerful weapon for reaching your goals, but I was able to build my business in five years by making better choices than most. I believe creative strategies are just as important as time, if not more so. I didn't want to wait thirty years to reach my goals, and I'm guessing you don't either. It's better to learn sound financial foresight today than to have 20/20 hindsight tomorrow.

> **Some people will tell you time is the most powerful weapon for reaching your goals, but I was able to build my business in five years by making better choices than most.**

The world of finance is complicated, and you are part of it whether you like it or not. Many people play from behind and feel the system is against them, while others learn the basic rules and achieve financial security late in life. However, some people learn the system and creative strategies to tip the odds in their favor. This book will share with you longstanding principles you need to know to achieve financial success, but more important, it will teach you that you don't have to settle for generic financial strategies.

I learned early on that generic wouldn't cut it. I grew up in a one-stoplight town in Oregon with a graduating high school class of around one hundred. There was a cow pasture next to the baseball field, and I bucked hay in the summer. Multiple father figures entered and exited my life, which led to a lot of moving and constant change. Money was tight all the time, and I thought that was just the way things were. I developed a mindset that good things don't happen to people like us. My financial goals were to make enough money someday that I could fill up my gas tank and check out at the grocery store without stress.

We worked hard but couldn't seem to get ahead. My mom raised four kids essentially on her own. We helped when we could, but it was a daily battle. To me as a child, the world of money seemed like a boxing match, and not one you could ever truly win. Each month, you would step in the ring with Mike Tyson and hope to make it to the next round still breathing. As I grew older and more aware, I noticed that some people had achieved financial success and peace of mind. What did they know that we didn't? They certainly did not work harder than we did. I decided to learn more about the world of finance and figure out why some had learned how to succeed while many others had not. I asked questions and interviewed successful people to learn about their mindset toward money and how they had achieved a higher level of financial success. I discovered that most didn't work *harder* than my family; they worked *smarter*. They learned lessons earlier than most and avoided "wish I knew that sooner" moments much more often.

I studied finance and economics in college to learn as much as I could about financial systems and how to make money work for me. My driving motivation was my mom and three sisters. I had watched our family struggle for many years and believed I had the power to do something about it. The first obstacle was to convince myself that a kid with an attitude problem from a small town and a broken home was capable and even worthy of financial success. Fortunately, the more people I met, the more I realized others had overcome much larger obstacles than I had and found financial success. So now that I knew it was possible, the hard work began. I had to learn how to do it.

I studied harder and talked to more people. I learned about necessary and established financial principles, but while my confidence rose, I was also disheartened. Many people shared some great financial nuggets but followed them up by saying if I did those things for the next thirty years, I could eventually retire and live comfortably. I couldn't wait that long! I wanted to help my mom and sisters now, and I wanted to experience financial security and give back while I was young.

After working as a financial advisor for a few years, I decided to start my own firm at the age of twenty-five. I learned that much of the financial industry focused on selling products as opposed to giving unbiased advice. It made sense. Financial professionals must earn a living like everyone else, so they try to find a product that will pay them while also solving a problem for the client. But I didn't want to be a salesperson. I committed to building a company that would consult clients on wise financial decisions whether it paid us or not. My mission was to bring creativity back to the financial industry and help as many people as possible avoid the financial regrets that come from wishing they would have known sooner. I studied relentlessly and ground my way into the upper ranks of the financial industry to challenge the status quo of financial planning.

At age twenty-eight, I earned a seat on my organization's chairman's council, which included the top 2% of advisors across the country. At age thirty, I made the "40 under 40 list," *InvestmentNews's* top forty financial advisors in the country under age forty. I have also coached hundreds of other advisors on how they can create a business that focuses on unbiased, creative financial advice.

My team, Legacy, is in the business of creative financial strategies. Our clients hold true to enduring principals, but we take it to the next level. I have advised thousands of people and hundreds of businesses over the years, and the feedback we hear most is "I wish I knew that sooner."

My mission is to give you a peek into our playbook. I will open your mind to strategies that only a small percentage of people know about and utilize to supercharge their financial plans.

THE MISSING PIECE: THE RIGHT INFORMATION AT THE RIGHT TIME

Everyone has the desire for financial success, so why is it such an elusive goal? Why can't people just set a goal to be wealthy? Part of the problem is that you first need to have the financial means to plan and save, and then you need to have the information necessary to respond at every twist and turn in the market. It requires a perfect storm of means *and* a plan, *and* the knowledge. It requires many pieces of the puzzle lining up at the right time. As a result, many people do nothing. The leading cause of wishing you had known that sooner is not having a plan and just hoping it all works out.

Financial success requires desire, means, and accurate information at the time you need it. I wrote this book to give you information that will make you think, alter decisions, and create a brighter financial future. But it's going to take more than a financial advisor hitting a magic button to meet all your monetary goals. If only it were that easy. Just as professional poker players can't control the cards they're dealt, nobody, including financial advisors, can control the markets. However, professional poker players do have an edge over average players, but it's not because of predictions, emotions, or hope. Instead, they make better decisions than others based on the cards they're holding. They know strategies that tip the odds in their favor and lead to much better results. They also have a much clearer view of the big picture and know most people play using the wrong strategies. The pros are willing to fold a decent hand when the odds are too great for a big loss. They know it's a long-run game, and results will come over time. They also know when to go all in.

Financial strategies work the same way. People often find their investments didn't perform as expected, college for their kids is more expensive than planned, Social Security isn't paying as much as they hoped, incomes are lower, and budgets are over. There's nothing you can do about it, but you can alter your strategies, assuming you know what to do. Some choices are good, some bad, and others are just plain awful. Unfortunately, the bad choices are often those that seem to make the most sense when your emotions are in control. However, wise financial choices, not emotions, are what make money. Wishing you had known sooner isn't a wise choice, and once you realize that regret, it may be too late.

As a financial advisor, I find nothing more painful than discovering a new client's financial picture would be far brighter had they taken different steps years earlier. It might be something as simple as checking off a different box on a Social Security document, using a Roth IRA (individual retirement account) over a traditional IRA, or using home equity to pay off high-interest-rate debt. If you're saving for retirement, the choices you make today can amount to making—or missing—millions of dollars.

> **If you're saving for retirement, the choices you make today can amount to making—or missing—millions of dollars.**

If you're looking for ways to improve your financial future, you need to learn certain strategies for achieving financial success and eliminating financial regrets. And you need to learn them now—not wish you had known them sooner.

We all know that to be a great athlete you must train hard, eat well, and develop your confidence. But how do great athletes beat the rest? Consider the level of talent at the Ironman triathlon competitions. Every athlete there is at an otherworldly fitness level, and all worked incredibly hard to get there. But the best know more than the rest. They know how to transition faster from the swim to the bike to shave precious seconds off their time. They know when and what type of food to eat during the race, what gear to use, even how to sleep to glean their bodies' maximum performance.

The most successful competitors don't simply follow an "average" training regimen and hope it works out on race day. The same is true with financial strategies. Most people will not argue that basic financial principles will help you be successful, but few people are familiar with strategies that will separate you from the pack. When it comes to your financial race, you only get one shot, and the stakes are too high to wish you had known sooner.

If you want to get better faster, you need to fix things you're doing wrong, not praise what you're doing right. Take the path of *most* resistance. Make a vow to lean into the discomfort and do the hard stuff. It might require making big changes, but a life goal is something worth doing.

What continues driving me today is the understanding that good decisions and intentional planning not only make my life better but give me the ability to change the lives of those I care about. Taking care of yourself is motivating, but people tend to quit on themselves when they get comfortable, while falling far short of their full potential. What could you do for your community or your family if your income doubled tomorrow or your financial decisions resulted in more money than you need in retirement?

We all have regrets. The key is realizing it doesn't have to happen again, and you can leverage regrets into a huge positive. Reflect back to the compounding effect of "wish I knew sooner." If you had made x decision one year earlier, what difference would that have made? Let's say you invested wisely for thirty years between the ages of thirty-five and sixty-five; an extra year of compounding makes a huge difference. That's a big deal and can be the difference between retiring five years early, putting your kids through college, or buying that dream home.

Imagine a circle that represents all the knowledge you need to achieve all your financial goals. Now, draw a smaller circle within that circle that represents the knowledge you have now. Everyone's circle should be fairly small, and the point is, there is knowledge that you currently don't have that is available to you, that you need to achieve your financial goals. So go get it!

If I told you I knew something that would make you $10 million, what could stand in your way from finding it? You would probably go to great lengths and do things you would have never done before. What is stopping you now? This book will help you understand there is a lot you don't know, but that information is necessary to make better financial decisions.

You are capable of far more than you know, and the stakes are too high for you not to act. The effects of dwelling on "would have, could have" can be much more detrimental than you think, and the longer you wait, the worse it might become. I urge you to not take this lightly. Doing so will almost guarantee you'll look back on your life and think, "I wish I knew that sooner."

In the chapters to come, I will show you powerful financial principles and introduce you to the creative side of financial planning.

You are not alone when you have the feeling of wishing you had understood finance sooner. I've worked with small business owners, millionaires, and billionaires who share that sentiment. Now I'm going to teach you to ask better questions and be more aware, so you can make better decisions.

Let's start by looking at the mindset of money. Changing your financial future really does start right there.

CHAPTER 1

YOLO Balance: Mindset of Money

A t age eighteen, John D. Rockefeller had no money. One day, he found an apple lying in the street. He polished it and sold it for fifty cents to a man walking down the road. John took that money, bought two apples for twenty-five cents each, and resold them for one dollar to another man standing on the curb. With that dollar, he bought four more apples and resold them to yet another man for two dollars. At age nineteen, he inherited millions of dollars from his grandmother.

Okay, sorry, it's not a true story but an old finance joke that shows how many millionaires and billionaires actually made their money. Unfortunately for the rest of us, it's not the common road to riches. So unless you have an ultra-rich relative, you must consider the second-best way of gaining wealth—saving and investing. No matter what your financial plans may be, whether saving for a home, sending kids to college, or securing a comfortable retirement, all financial plans begin with savings. There's just no way around the math—you can't save money you don't have. To get cash out, you must put cash in, even if it means having to polish a few apples.

Instead, people say they'll wait until the "time is right." Well, what does that mean? When you have tons of cash lying around, no expenses, and the kids have graduated from college? If you have those kinds of money "troubles," you wouldn't need to invest. Don't make the mistake of waiting for money to appear. If you're waiting for the right time to begin retirement planning, you're just planning to work longer. Today is the day to begin. It's uncomfortable, but remember, if you press into it, that's when the best things happen.

When it comes to investing, time is your best friend, so the sooner the dollars go to work, the more money you'll have in the future. However, your mindset can be one of the biggest challenges. It's hard to live for tomorrow and all too easy to live for today. To change your future, you must change your thinking.

YOU ONLY LIVE ONCE

Many people live by the YOLO rule—You Only Live Once. They'll say, "You can't take it with you, so you might as well enjoy it today." They'd rather buy the latest Lexus lined with Louis Vuitton seat covers than put money into an investment that will brighten their future. The YOLO lifestyle is easy to fall into, especially with key offenders urging you to buy today. I'm not going to mention any names, but they rhyme with Mastercard and Visa. Take a look at the message behind some of their slogans:

- It's your window to the things you want.
- Today's way to pay.
- More living. Fewer limits.
- Make life simple.

Americans are experts at spending, and it's one of the reasons why we barely make the top hundred countries ranked by savings rates. It's much easier to live by YOLO because you get immediate satisfaction. After all, you only live once.

Some people's YOLO lifestyle is fueled by concern with what others think, so they spend money on what marketing companies call conspicuous income—spending so that everyone else can see you've got money. Too many times, however, we're not buying the things we need, and sometimes not even the things we want, but instead, the things everybody else thinks we need.

If you want to live by YOLO, that's a personal choice, and I'm not going to say it's wrong. However, it does come with a warning: Don't expect the lottery to bail you out, don't hope that a rich grandmother will leave you a windfall, don't expect to make a fortune selling apples.

Social Security won't provide all your income needs either. Social Security was never intended to be a retirement plan, but instead, only a supplement. However, even those benefits are dwindling. In 2019, the administration reported that if nothing is done, starting in 2034, it will only be able to pay out 77% of promised benefits. The reality is the program's small role is getting even smaller. It may be social, but it's far from secure. Another concerning trend is bankruptcies in older age groups. A study by the Consumer Bankruptcy Project found that the number of people sixty-five and over filing for bankruptcy grew nearly 204% from 1991 to 2016, and the percentage of seniors among all US bankruptcy filers increased by nearly five times over the same period.[1] So what can you rely on? You can't treat your financial plans like an autonomous Tesla, put them on autopilot, and fall asleep. You must rely on you.

IT BEGINS WITH YOU

A change in your financial future begins with a change in your spending. If you have big financial plans, you must ditch the YOLO philosophy. It may be true that you only live once, but it's also true you can't spend the same dollar twice. Again, the math is inescapable: Money spent today can't be spent tomorrow. If you want more money in the future, you must spend less today.

While financial concepts and investment strategies matter, *you* are the biggest key to your success. Big financial plans usually entail long-term commitments, and knowledge of all the financial strategies in the world will do nothing unless you're willing to use them—and follow through with the plans.

While investing begins with you, it can also end with you. Unfortunately, for many people, events in their lives prevent them from getting started. They feel financially stuck. They can't find the money to invest each month and wouldn't know how to invest it even if they did. It's easier to just do nothing. Instead, they hope that one day, things will change. Hope is never a good strategy. Deciding to do nothing is worse.

If you've made bad financial decisions in the past, that's okay. They're your lessons. Let the future be your motivation. The present is your gift, and today is the day to make changes. Whether you're saving for a home, kids' college, retirement, or just a rainy day, you need to understand that every dollar you spend today reduces the amount you'll have in the future. If you want to save for the future, you can't spend like there's no tomorrow.

YOLO BALANCE

A key to good financial decisions is striking a life balance. Some investing books go to extremes and suggest living like a hermit and socking away every last dime so you can die wealthy. The better approach to investing—like anything else—is with balance. You can spend money on yourself, but there are smart ways and not-so-smart ways. Going on vacation may be an investment in yourself if it fuels you to be more productive. Buying a rental property in your favorite vacation spot is another example. Even buying and reading this book is an investment of money and time in yourself. All these decisions provide personal benefits but also create future wealth. Spending money on yourself isn't a bad thing, but always be sure to get something out of the deal. If you do, it can be money well spent.

While it's important to enjoy life now, you still must plan for your future, because the odds are dramatically in your favor to live into your seventies, and those odds are improving every year. For example, people in their thirties and forties today have nearly a 90% chance to live another thirty or more years. So why spend money and plan like you won't be around to enjoy it?

We need to enjoy our lives, and the ultimate goal isn't retirement, but rather financial freedom and independence. Whether you reach that at age forty, fifty-five, or sixty-five is up to you.

Let's put this into a different context. If I told you a particular investment had a 90% chance to turn $100 into $1,000,000 but a 10% chance of failure, how comfortable would you be with that bet? And how many $100 investments would you be willing to make?

The risk of missing out on a short-term $100 enjoyment is far outweighed by the future upside. "Wish I knew that sooner" financial moments are born of scenarios like this. Should you upgrade your car or TV again since it has been a few years, or should you first focus on funding your 401(k), Roth IRA, or paying down debt? Those small incremental decisions today make all the difference in your financial future.

I've always believed in investing in ourselves. Investing doesn't always mean buying stocks, bonds, or mutual funds. Your greatest asset is always your ability to make additional income or create new income. Choose to invest in *yourself* as well. Study new ways to think and create wealth, take online classes, attend seminars, or invest in a new business. My firm has many clients that invest little in the stock market because they've learned to invest in new businesses or real estate.

Some of the best investments I ever made were not in the stock market or real estate.

I follow the same mantra. Some of the best investments I ever made were not in the stock market or real estate. Instead, I made choices that would influence my future in a positive light:

- I paid $1,400 for a two-day intensive speaking course, which challenged me, made me a better speaker, and made me realize I'm capable of more than I thought I was capable of. It changed the course of my consulting and coaching career.

- I also paid $5,000 to take a Certified Financial Planner course, which dramatically increased my knowledge and confidence for starting my business. It's been responsible for a large portion of my income for the past eight years.

- A few years ago, I paid $900 to attend an industry conference that planted a seed that turned into a new revenue stream, increasing my company's revenue by more than 40%. Could I have invested this money in the stock market? Of course, but I doubt it would have paid the same dividends.

Just as many people fund their 401(k), Roth IRA, or make their mortgage payment each month, you should constantly invest in your future by investing in yourself. Find YOLO balance and enjoy life's little

moments now, but beware of YOLO's mischievous sidekick, FOMO—
Fear of Missing Out. It can be a formidable decision-making obstacle,
and you must understand that an expense creates a short-term benefit
but consumes value over time. Buying a new TV isn't the same as buying
a new computer for the same money. You may have different reasons
for buying things, just be sure YOLO isn't one of them.

NEEDS VERSUS WANTS

Financial success is about discipline. You must develop a different
mindset, and one of the most powerful is to question whether any
purchase is a need or a want. It sounds trivial, but it's one of the most
important steps for building a solid financial future. For most people,
daily purchases are insignificant, so they're never questioned. If they
are questioned, credit cards have the answer. We rarely say no to most
purchases. If we want it, we buy it.

Spending today, however, means it's money you can't spend in
the future. Rather than spending money today, just because you can
afford it, ask if it's something you can live without. Is it a need or a
want? Recognizing you could delay a purchase helps you realize it's
more of a want than a need because there's no urgency to have it. Life
will go on just fine without it.

Here are a couple of good reality checks. First, ask if a purchase
will solve a problem. How will it make you better off? If you can't
pinpoint a problem it's solving, then question the purchase.

On the other hand, if it's glaringly obvious that it's going to solve
an important problem, save money, save time, or make you more
productive with your job, it's probably a need. For instance, perhaps
you're considering a new computer. If your job requires you to crank
out a lot of production, but your current system is too slow, you could
argue that it's a need. You can put your finger on the problem it's going

to solve; you can see there would be a significant benefit.

Conversely, if you're buying it just because it's the newest technology and would be cool to have or just because it's on sale at a great price, that's a different story. Keep this distinction in mind, and you'll find that most things you're thinking of buying aren't really needs. If you can at least train yourself to do this small check, it greatly helps with all purchases—and therefore your financial future. Remember, you can't spend the same dollar twice.

A second test is to ask yourself what's going to change, and then see if it's worth the price. For instance, you may walk into a store on Black Friday and see a $2,000 television marked down to $1,500. If you feel you must buy it because you're saving so much money, ask what's going to change?

If you have a television sitting in the living room today but make the purchase anyway, you'll still have a television sitting in the same spot tomorrow. Nothing really changed, other than perhaps the screen size or technology. Don't look at it as though you're saving $500; ask if these minor changes are worth spending $1,500. That's all that's changing, so that's what the decision boils down to. Or maybe you found a new Louis Vuitton purse for $3,000. It's the newest model, it's flashy, it's beautiful—and you must have it. And why not? You only live once. Well, before you whip out the Mastercard to give you more living with lower credit limits, ask what's going to change? You have a purse now, and you'll have one after. The only thing that'll change is perhaps the color or size. It's not a question of whether you can afford it. Instead, ask if it'll be worth spending $3,000 to gain an insignificant benefit when that same money would create an enormous benefit in the future. Change your mindset to question every purchase to see if it's a need or want. Different perspectives lead to different decisions, but they must be made, because you can't spend the same dollar twice.

The Five-Day Rule

One way to rein in errant spending is to adopt the Five-Day Rule. We have all made emotional purchases and would admit to spending money on things we know we don't need. I'm not here to tell you to give up expensive coffee, nice vacations, and eating out in pursuit of saving a million dollars by age sixty. But I do want to help you understand the true cost of the YOLO approach toward money.

> I'm not here to tell you to give up expensive coffee, nice vacations, and eating out in pursuit of saving a million dollars by age sixty. But I do want to help you understand the true cost of the YOLO approach toward money.

Think of nonessential purchases as those that just improve upon something you already have or are a luxury version of an essential item. Before making a nonessential or impulse purchase, wait at least five days. This rule does not tell you that you can't buy those items, but it does give your mind a little extra time to calculate the true cost and feel more confident about whether the item is a need or a want.

Using the Five-Day Rule can make a significant impact on your spending. Research commissioned by Ladder and conducted by OnePoll[2] shows the average American spends approximately $1,500 per month on nonessential items, or $18,000 per year. A supporting study shows about $5,400 of that are impulse buys. Imagine if you reduced nonessential spending by 40% per year. With these figures, you'd save about $7,200 per year. What could you do with that money?

In less than three years' time, you could save a down

payment to purchase a $200,000 piece of real estate. Let's assume that property generates $1,200 per month in rent, and your monthly mortgage payment is $900. Assuming a thirty-year mortgage, in thirty years, you will have a paid-off property that even in a slow market could increase in value to $400,000. In addition to the $400,000 from the sale of the home in thirty years, you collected a minimum of $108,000 in excess rent. Reducing nonessential spending by 40% for just three years turned it into more than $500,000 in your pocket.

Invest $7,200 each year for four years, assuming a 9% return (slightly below the long-term average); then, let it sit for twenty years. It nets $185,000.

You could also use the funds to start a new business with the potential for an enormously profitable future. RxBar, for instance, was started with a $10,000 investment and later sold for $600 million.

Saving the additional income per year is the first step. Making the money work for you is a totally different story. Many people do not have the experience or desire to develop, implement, and monitor financial strategies like this on their own. They don't start saving or planning because they don't know where to begin. The good news is you don't have to. My team can help you navigate the information and put a plan into action, avoid regrets in your life, and make better financial decisions. If you think incrementally, you'll realize just how expensive errant spending can be.

BE CAREFUL OF INVESTING TIME

I met a client once who owned bank stock for years and years. What started as a local bank was bought multiple times until it was part of Wachovia. This client had a majority of her wealth in Wachovia stock and would not diversify out of it because it had done so well for her for so long. She had a loyalty to the stock, but the company did not share that loyalty. Wachovia later went bankrupt, and this client lost over $10 million. Just because you don't buy something or you decide to sell it does not make that investment bad; it just means it is best for your situation to part ways at that particular time.

This woman invested so much time into this investment, she felt she couldn't back out. If you decide it's not going to solve a problem and isn't worth the money for the small changes it'll make, stop investing time. If you're on the fence about a decision, it's an immediate indication that it's a want, not a need. Still, it's tempting to go back to the store or the website and look at it over and over, day after day, again and again. Each trip, you're trying to resolve the issue of whether or not to buy. The problem with spending so much time is that it becomes a mental "cost," and the more time you invest, the more likely you are to buy it. If you don't buy it, you'll feel as if you "wasted" all that time, so it only makes sense to buy it.

This mental accounting trap is a trick car salespeople use by trying to get you to invest a lot of time with them. If you walk on the lot, ask a couple of questions, and leave, it's easy to forget about your quick stop and never give it a second thought. But if they can get you to spend a lot of time there, it's harder and harder to walk away from a new set of wheels. If they can get you to spend hours there, walking, talking, and looking, they're swinging the odds in their favor. So once you decide something isn't a need, drop it. Don't spend time on things you originally determined weren't worth your time.

The same holds true for simply waiting in line. Georgetown University studied the scenario of sunk costs—the cost of something that already happened that you can't get back.[3] The study specifically looked at the impulse to purchase something after spending an inordinate length of time waiting in line. It might not be what you came for, but you buy something anyway, in a sort of retail spite, to make up for standing there so long.

You can't gain and apply knowledge once time has passed. Remember, you only live once, so don't miss the chance to invest in yourself. Doing so significantly boosts your ability to make better financial choices. On the other hand, failing to challenge yourself and learn more is one of the major influencers of "wish I knew that sooner" moments. Time is one of your greatest assets. Don't waste it. The health of your future self and those you care about depend on it.

Now that we've looked at mindset, I want to share some fundamentals, but only the ones that work for my clients, colleagues, and me. You're going to hear a lot from various "experts" about financial fundamentals, but the good news is, there are some basic truths that are undebatable. In fact, I've found that if people try to debate the validity of these truths, they usually have something to sell you.

Chapter 1 Summary

1. **Make sure you apply YOLO the right way.** You only live once, so do your future self a favor and take control of your finances now.

2. **Understand the difference between a need and a want.** That's fundamental to successful financial planning. Train your mind to run quick math to understand the true cost of "wants" before you buy them.

3. **Use the Five-Day Rule,** a great tool to help retrain your mind and reduce the lifetime cost of impulse purchases.

4. **Remember sunk costs,** and do not let time invested into a decision determine the outcome. You should always evaluate financial decisions with a clean slate.

CHAPTER 2

Undebatable Fundamentals

The first time I went to Disney World, we didn't plan it very well and just hoped things would work out. We ended up standing in line for hours while people who had planned ahead and had the right strategies took the fast-pass line and waited for only ten minutes. As I learned in that situation, the right strategies fast-track your success. And I believe the following fundamentals are essential for anyone to achieve financial success.

NOTHING IS EASY

Nobody wants to say they're the master at stuff anyone can do. The world thrives on competition, and if there's one arena that's bombarded with contestants, it's investing. It's the one field that absolutely will touch you at some point in your life. However, you ultimately dictate the success. The best coaches in the world can't produce a successful athlete if that person doesn't want to put in the work. You can lead a horse to water, and well, you know the rest. So the first thing to realize is that successful investing is all about you. A financial mentor can work wonders; however, it doesn't work the other way around. Don't expect to hire a financial planner who can hit the "magic button" and flood your account with money. They're financial planners, not the Federal Reserve.

Of all the moving parts involved with investing, you're the only irreplaceable piece of the puzzle. Think about that before you get started. Is it really what you want to do? I'm not talking about for the next thirty days or even the next two or three. That's about the extent of most people's attention span for investing, and if they haven't been able to retire in five years at the age of thirty, they figure investing just doesn't work. No one looks back on their life and wishes they had tried less, slept longer, played more video games, or known about the fundamentals of investing ten years later. Start with the proper mindset: Nothing is easy. That is, nothing is easy if it's worth doing. The goal is to get in the fast-pass line.

> New investors often think consistency means you must pick winning stocks far more often than not. In my opinion, people need to make good decisions more often than not, and it is not about stock picking.

STAY FOCUSED

Investing requires consistency. However, consistency comes in many forms. New investors often think consistency means you must pick winning stocks far more often than not. Instead, people need to make good decisions more often than not, and it is not about stock picking. It is about consistent good decisions and strategies. A good plan will help you gain financial independence whether you own Apple stock, Netflix, or only invest in real estate.

You must also be consistent in your decisions. A lot of financial plans can work, but few will result in success if you're constantly changing the plan. If you're committed to a financially successful future and retirement, you must have consistency in some part of the plan. This is where financial planners can be worth their weight in gold, because they can help you see financial goals through unbiased eyes. Just as an attorney who represents himself has a fool for a client, investors who try to go about the long, hard road alone face much bigger challenges than necessary. It's not necessarily because you can't create a plan or pick stocks, but it's because you're likely not to stay consistent.

FUNDAMENTALS MATTER MORE

For any endeavor, there's a difference between fundamentals and style. Fundamentals are those things that are absolutely essential for success. They're common to all. Styles, on the other hand, are techniques that people adopt to make fundamentals more comfortable. Take a look at pro golfers, for instance. On one hand, every player's swing looks a lot like the others. Head down, steady swing, weight transfer through the ball, and so on. Those are the fundamentals.

At the same time, none of them look exactly alike. Those are style differences, and they're just things that allow players to be more consistent in carrying out the fundamentals. Investing is the same way. Some people may be more comfortable investing in an S&P 500 index fund while other may wish to use the Nasdaq 100. Others may wish to select their own stocks. Those are style differences, and all investors could do equally well. So the first fundamental idea is to realize there are a million ways to approach investing—different styles—and that's one of the reasons it can seem so overwhelming. But the styles aren't what matter most. To be successful with investing, you must focus on the fundamentals, and that's what I'll be showing you later in the book. Good financial planners, however, will help you settle on a style that fits your personality and risk tolerances. A good investing style makes the long, hard road much easier. It makes fundamentals more comfortable, and that means better consistency.

AVOID NEVER-ENDING SPENDING

It should go without saying, but if you're going to invest money, you must have money to invest. And that means you can't spend more than you make. It's painfully obvious, so why is it taking up space in an investing book?

Because it's one of the most consistent problems among investors. It's easy to build up a mountain of debt because we're bombarded with ads convincing us why we should have this or can't live without that. People get themselves into lifestyles where they're working to just service the debt. All their money goes toward things they've bought in the past, and that means none goes toward the future. Always consider your future self. Be willing to make sacrifices today to live the life you want tomorrow.

CHEAPER DOESN'T MEAN BETTER

The other day, I took my car to get the oil changed, and in the mechanic's garage, I spotted a sign: *If you want it good and cheap, it won't be fast. If you want it fast and good, it won't be cheap. And if you want it cheap and fast, it won't be good.* It's a clever way to show there's always a trade-off between cost, quality, and time. However, when it comes to financial advice and products, people often lose sight of these connections and just hunt for the cheapest they can find. The problem is that financial products can hide fees in many places. A firm that charges little for advice may be charging the most for products.

So while it may seem like you're saving a lot, those fees can eat into your returns over decades, costing you tens of thousands of dollars.

Quality also costs money, and for financial advisors, that comes with experience. The advisors who have solid track records will also have long lines of clients, and the only way to equalize those lines is through higher prices. Would you pay a 50% fee if someone tripled your money? Of course you would. In the absence of value, fees are a concern. Low fees are fine as long as you're not settling for cheap advice.

EMOTIONS ARE NOT YOUR FRIEND

Consistency is critical for success, but it's hard to be consistent when you're emotional about money. Don't think you're not. It's widely known that investors are notoriously risk averse, which means they despise taking losses. In fact, they'll take additional risks in hopes of avoiding a loss. It's more than just a theory, and there's even a budding financial field called "behavioral finance" that centers on the inconsistencies of investors because of the psychology of investing. In 2002, Daniel Kahneman won the Nobel Prize in Economics for the psychology of judgment and decision making. One experiment Kahneman had done was to ask thousands of respondents which they would prefer: Receive $500 cash guaranteed or flip a coin and receive $1,000 if heads and nothing if tails. Which sounds best to you?

If you're like 99% of the respondents, you chose the $500 guaranteed cash. Both choices are expected to return $500, but the coin flip has risk. In other words, if you could flip the coin thousands of times, half the time you'd win $1,000 and half the time you'd win nothing. On average, you'd win $500 each flip. However, taking the for-sure cash always returns $500. Because investors wish to avoid risk, the majority take the for-sure $500. That's not so hard to understand, but it's also not where the experiment got interesting.

Kahneman reversed the question: Would you prefer to take a $500 for-sure loss? Or flip a coin for a $1,000 loss if heads, and no loss if tails? If investors are risk averse, they should always be risk averse and choose the $500 for-sure loss. They shouldn't choose a path that may make things go from bad to worse if they don't like losing money. But they didn't. Instead, they chose the coin toss to gamble their way from a losing situation. It shows that investors aversion to loss is so great that it overrides their aversion to risk. In other words, they're willing to take more risk if it means they might escape a loss. Talk about a dangerous combination for investing. Think about the tech-wreck of 2000, the 2008 financial meltdown, the 20% drop in the fourth quarter of 2018, and more recently, the COVID-19 pandemic in mid-2020. They were all fast, aggressive drops where most investors took large losses during the panics. The right move was to be buying. However, emotions rarely let you make the best decisions when dealing with money. For investors, emotions are not your friend, but a great financial planner can help you develop the necessary nerves of steel.

Every investment has risk, potential reward, and fees. Make sure you understand all three before you decide to buy.

RISK, REWARD, AND FEES: WHERE ONE IS, THE OTHER TWO WILL FOLLOW

Let's get straight to the point. Every investment has risk, potential reward, and fees. Make sure you understand all three before you decide to buy.

When people talk about risk, it means there's potential for a bad outcome. However, there are varying degrees of risk. There's risk in driving to Starbucks, and there's risk in skydiving. Whether you need a shot of caffeine or adrenaline, there must be something that makes the actions worthwhile. Otherwise, why take the risk?

Investing works the same way. For some investments, there's a good chance for things to go wrong—losing lots of money—and they're obviously considered high risk. For others, there's no chance of losing money, and they're called risk-free investments. However, even "risk-free" investments could lose value because of inflation or some other form of risk. Most investments fall somewhere between these two extremes. You're probably wondering why anyone would put money into a risky investment if there are risk-free choices available.

That's where the risk-reward connection comes in. While risky investments may lose a lot of money, they may also make a lot of money. Risk-free investments, on the other hand, aren't ever going to make you rich.

While risk and reward can be difficult to understand at times, they are usually part of the conversation. The "fee" conversation is usually a different story. This can be brushed over or hidden in the small print. People who advertise low-risk investments that have great potential for big returns and very low fees are probably trying to sell you something. As I mentioned earlier, cheaper does not always mean better. Good advice will come with a fee. The goal should be that it is a win-win for all parties, and it should be out in the open.

If someone tries to convince you that they have a low-risk investment that has a great potential for return and very low fees, they are probably trying to sell you something.

ASYMMETRIC RISK: TIP THE ODDS IN YOUR FAVOR

For any investment, be sure there's more potential for upside gains than downside losses, or what's called an asymmetric trade-off in risk and reward. Tony Robbins's book, *Unshakeable: Your Guide to Financial Freedom*, goes into great detail about this.

Most seasoned investors will not settle for a 1:1 ratio of return to risk, and even a 2:1 ratio may not satisfy them. Some of the biggest names such as Warren Buffett or Paul Tudor Jones look for a 5:1 or even 6:1 ratio. This means, when they invest $1, they expect an opportunity to turn it into $5 or $6. At this rate, you only have to pick correctly 20% of the time to stay even. If you invest $1 in five different opportunities, four of them could go to zero and if the fifth returned five times, you will be back at $5.

Unfortunately, most of us are not buying or starting companies to achieve these returns like many large investors. So how can the rest of us achieve asymmetric risk and reward? You need to learn to buy the dips. For example, we helped our clients buy undervalued stocks during the housing crisis in 2007 and the COVID pandemic in 2020. Companies such as Lowe's, General Motors, and even the S&P 500 index were undervalued and on sale.

Lowes stock was around $126 in early 2020, fell to around $60, and later recovered to $171. If you purchased near the bottom, your return would be near 185%.

General Motors stock was worth near $37 but fell to around $14. It recovered to $37 later in the year. That would have been close to a 164% return.

The S&P 500 index was around 3,393 and plummeted to around 2,191 and later recovered to 3,463 and counting. That would have been close to a 60% rate of return in a matter of months not including dividends.

If investors avoid big mistakes and losses and learn to take advantage of market dips, they will reach their goals much quicker.

MAXIMIZE THE POWER OF COMPOUNDING

No matter how much financial planners try to drive home the power of compounding, investors never appreciate it, and that's why so many bail on their investment plans after a short time. It's understandable because it's not easy to see why it works—or why it's so powerful. To appreciate the power, imagine doing the following experiment. In step one, start with a sheet of paper. For step two, place two sheets on top. For step three, place four sheets on top. With each step, you'll double the number of sheets in the previous step and add to the stack. How tall is the stack after fifty steps? Most people can't see how it would be much taller than forty or fifty feet. A few who go out on a limb may guess it's the height of a skyscraper. Not even close. It would reach to the sun—ninety-three million miles away. It's a fascinating look at compounding, because a single sheet of paper is so thin. Doubling it even ten or twenty times doesn't seem like it would have much effect. In fact, it doesn't. Like most compounding, it's the final steps where the force kicks in. For example, while it takes fifty steps to reach the sun, just one more step would bring you all the way back to Earth. Compounding is the trick to making long-term investing work. If you're trying to save a million dollars for retirement in thirty years, you may feel like you're far behind after twenty years. But that's because you're not allowing for the compounding forces to kick in. It's the final five years or so where the true power begins to show. Compounding reinforces the idea of why it's so crucial to stick with the plan.

COMPOUND INTEREST MYTH

Unfortunately, compound interest can also be used, whether intentional or not, to set unrealistic expectations. Many financial projections models use a consistent rate of return when illustrating the power of compound interest. For instance, planners may say the market has returned 10%, on average, over the last fifty years, so let's use that for our projects. Or, they'll say let's use 8% to be conservative. It gives the illusion that you're guaranteed to hit your goals just because you're using a lower number than the average. No matter which number you choose, it will always result in impressive outcomes because of compounding. Unfortunately, investments never go up by a steady amount each year, even if you're using a conservative estimate. The problem is that planners like to add percentages, so for instance, say an investment steadily returns 20% gains followed by 18% losses. Most financial planners would say it's an average gain of 2%. Just use the conservative number of 2%, multiply it out by the number of years, and you've got your retirement number, right?

Wrong.

If you earn 20% in one year and lose 18% the next, you're down 1.6%. And the longer you stay in the investment, the worse it gets. After ten years, you've eroded 15% of your money. Good financial planning requires stress testing, and that's what my firm does, by considering many types of outcomes based on historical returns. We include the good and bad years—not the average—to see what's most likely to occur. I don't know what the market will return, or when the bad years will strike, but I am confident that any investment you own will not go up by the same percentage every year.

These are the foundational principles I think you should understand before we go to the next step. Now, that we've covered them, let's begin to increase the creativity in our strategies—starting with debt.

Chapter 2 Summary

1. **Financial success is not easy.** If it were, everyone would have it. When you go to the gym and lift weights, they are supposed to be heavy. If something is hard, it does not mean you are doing it wrong.

2. **Cheaper doesn't mean better.** Be aware of fees and expenses, but don't get caught in the trap that fees should be a dominant factor in your decision making when investing money or paying for advice. The main measures should be value and results.

3. **Emotions are not your friend.** It is widely understood that emotions tend to cause people to buy high when they feel good and sell low when they feel bad or scared. Don't fall into that trap.

4. **Asymmetric risk:** The most successful investors focus on the relationship between upside potential and downside risk. Don't risk a dollar to make a dollar. Find ways to reduce your risk so your upside meaningfully exceeds your downside risk.

5. **Compound interest myth:** Don't use a constant rate of return when projecting retirement or investment growth. Historically, the stock market has not returned the same rate of return each year. You need to use a variable rate of return to get a more realistic projection.

The questions may already be swirling in your head and you want to take action to improve your financial plan. I encourage you to finish the entire book, but you can reach out to my team to learn how your financial plan can be improved.

InvestLegacy.com

CHAPTER 3

The Positive
Power of Debt

I f debt didn't exist, no one would own a house or a business. Without debt, nearly all the giant publicly traded corporations you use every day such as Apple, Amazon, and Google would have never been created. To be blunt, the economy might not even exist. However, for many people, debt is viewed as a negative thing, and many spend too much time paying down debt when their time would be better served focusing on other financial strategies. To get ahead with your financial plan, you must understand that debt is a tool, and used wisely, it can be a path to success. Like anything else in life, it's about balance. If you're better off because of your car and home, and major corporations provide useful products, services—and jobs—and the investors who loaned the money are better off from the interest, it's hard to say that debt is evil.

WHAT YOU MAY NOT KNOW ABOUT DEBT

You may carry a lot of debt but routinely pay it off every three or four months. That's not a problem. It also depends on the type of debt. If most of your debt is in your mortgage, that's one thing. There's a real asset backing it up, and it will likely appreciate over time. How can you check if your debt levels are too high? There are several helpful calculations to find out.

First, check your debt-income ratio, which is found by dividing your total monthly debt by your total gross income. For example, let's say you add up all your credit card payments, house payment, car payments, etc. for the month, and it comes up to $2,000, but your income is $5,000 per month. Your debt-income ratio is $2,000 ÷ $5,000, or 40%. Most financial experts suggest a maximum of 30% to 40%. However, keep in mind that 43% is generally the highest ratio you can have to qualify for a mortgage. If you're thinking of shopping for a home or financing big-ticket items such as a car or boat, you should first work on getting your debt-income ratio down. Otherwise, assuming you even get the loan, you'll end up with a higher interest rate, and that can add up to tens of thousands of dollars—or hundreds of thousands—over the life of the loan.

Another test is to make sure your credit utilization ratio is below 30%, which is a calculation specific to credit cards. If you don't know your ratio, you can sign up on free websites and phone apps like CreditKarma.com, CreditSesame.com, or NerdWallet.com to get free credit scores. Most credit card scoring models, such as FICO and VantageScore 3.0, calculate your credit utilization ratio, which is the amount of current credit card debt divided by the total spending limit. You're in the safest zone if your ratio is 9% or below. For example, if you have $10,000 in total spending limits, whether it's for one card or several, but you currently have a total of $900 charged, then you're

THE POSITIVE POWER OF DEBT

in the "green" zone with a utilization ratio of 9%.

The next tier that's still considered acceptable is 10% to 29%, so if you have $2,900 in debt, you're still safe but pushing the green-zone boundaries. Between 30% and 49%, you're in the yellow zone, and you'll definitely see your credit score take a sharp decline once you cross the 30% mark. From 50% to 74%, the needle's pushing the orange zone, and above 75%, you're definitely in the red zone.

It's important to understand that even if your utilization ratio is low, you can still have a negative impact to your score if a single card exceeds 30%. Let's say you have several cards with a total of $30,000 spending limits, and none carry any balances. However, you have one card with a $1,000 spending limit. If you charge $600 on it, and take time to pay it off, your overall credit utilization ratio will be low, $600 ÷ $30,000, or 2%. However, that one card is at 60%, and that will severely impact your credit score. If you're going to carry a balance, try to use the cards that have the highest credit limits. So, your credit utilization is another gauge of whether you have too much credit card debt. If it's exceeding 30%, you need to bring it down. It's not necessarily that 30% is a high debt-income ratio, but it's because the interest rates are so high that it poses a big danger. Of course, you must keep things in perspective. If you have one card with a $1,000 limit, and you're carrying a $500 balance, your credit utilization ratio may look high at 50%, but it's still only $500, so it's not a big risk.

> It's important to understand that even if your utilization ratio is low, you can still have a negative impact to your score if a single card exceeds 30%.

MONEY DOESN'T KNOW THE DIFFERENCE

One of the biggest reasons people get stuck in debt is because they incorrectly prioritize debts as either "good debt" or "bad debt." For example, people find it better to send extra money each month toward their mortgage because it's good debt. A home is usually their biggest asset, a place to live, and something that'll grow in value. They're expecting to make a lot of money from it, so focusing on paying it off seems like a better use of money. To make those extra payments, however, they pay the minimums on credit cards because that's bad debt. It was just for stuff they never really wanted, emergency repairs, or other things that are never going to appreciate in value, so why rush to throw money away?

Instead of thinking about "good or bad" debt, realize that debt is debt. Money doesn't know the difference, but you should. It's up to you to put money where it's treated best. Get rid of expensive debts first—the ones carrying the highest interest rates—even if it means making minimum payments to your mortgage or not putting money away toward savings. Mathematically, you'll be better off compared to any other choices, which means you'll have more money in the future. It makes no sense to aggressively try to pay down a mortgage at 5% interest when you're paying 20% interest on credit cards. That's a 15% leak in your financial boat, and if you're trying to save for the future, you can't afford any leaks, much less double-digit ones. Similarly, it doesn't make sense to sock money away into a savings account or CD earning 1% while floating 20% credit card debt—that's a 19% leak.

If you have $5,000 in a savings account and $5,000 in credit card debt, you're better off using the savings to pay off the debt and then pay yourself back. Now the interest goes to you—not the bank. However, don't deplete all your savings to pay off debt. It's a good idea to keep at least six months' worth of living expenses in cash. If you should lose your job, you don't want added pressures of trying to meet the next mortgage payment.

What if you have no savings but large consumer debts? If debts are large enough, consider taking a home equity loan to pay off the debt. It's a strategy most people would never consider because they think they're using "good debt" to pay off "bad debt." They feel their equity would be missing out on any appreciation in the home's value. After all, if real estate values are rising—and they typically do—aren't you making yourself worse off by taking money from your home's equity? Well, your home's equity isn't as profitable as you think.

YOUR HOME'S EQUITY EARNS NOTHING

It's hard to believe, but your home's equity earns nothing. That's right. It's money just sitting there, doing nothing. It's no different than if you had it stuffed under your mattress. How is that possible? If your home's value is rising, isn't your equity earning those gains? Why waste it on paying off high debts?

Your equity is simply the difference between the home's market value and what's owed on the mortgage. Equity can be thought of as "what you own" minus "what you owe." If you "own" a $500,000 home but owe $400,000, your equity is $100,000. In other words, if you sold the home and paid off the mortgage, you'd be left with $100,000.

Now let's say the home's value rises to $550,000 next year. Ignoring the small decline in your mortgage balance, your equity has increased to $550,000 – $400,000, or $150,000. It looks like your $100,000 equity earned $50,000 for doing nothing, so taking equity out seems like it could be an expensive decision. Where else are you going to earn 50% on your money? Well, how would things have changed if you had no equity? In other words, a $500,000 home with a $500,000 mortgage? Would you have earned nothing?

If the home's value rises to $550,000, your equity is now $550,000 – $500,000, or $50,000. The equity still increased by $50,000. Pick any amount of starting equity, and you'll see that with the home at $550,000, the equity increases by the same $50,000. Home equity appreciation has nothing to do with the amount of equity you started with. Instead, it simply depends on the increases in the home's value, and that's up to the market to decide—not your equity.

This doesn't mean there aren't advantages to paying off your home. Sure, all things being equal, you'd like to get rid of that debt because the sooner it's gone, the sooner those payments and the interest stays in your pocket. But remember, debt is debt, and money doesn't know the difference. As long as you have debts to pay, you might as well pay them off in the most efficient way. Whether it's credit card debt, student loans, medical bills, or any others, you want to pay off the ones with the highest interest rates first. If debt levels are high enough, it'll pay to use cheap money to pay off expensive debt.

If you have $20,000 in credit card debt at 20% interest, you'll benefit by taking $20,000 from your home's equity to instantly patch that financial hole.

Just as with the previous example where you delayed putting money into a savings account to focus on paying off the $5,000 credit card debt, you'll get the same benefit by taking out a home equity loan to pay off high-interest-rate debt. If you have $20,000 in credit card debt at 20% interest, you'll benefit by taking $20,000 from your home's equity to instantly patch that financial hole. Now, you'll have two advantageous choices. First, you can continue making the same payments you would have been making for the credit card, but at least you're saving the difference in interest charges. If your credit card charges 20%, and your home equity loan is 5%, you're saving the 15% difference. Second, you could make smaller payments to pay off the home equity loan and put the difference into another financial plan, perhaps saving for retirement.

The most effective financial plans use debt wisely. In addition, many of the plans I help clients build make it a goal to eliminate or pay down debt before retirement. What season are you in? Is it time to harness the power of debt to make it work for you, or is it time to eliminate debt? One is not better than the other. Focus on what is most impactful for you.

Chapter 3 Summary

1. **Debt is not bad.** Debt is a tool like any other tool. Cars are a great tool, but if used incorrectly they can cause major damage. Respect debt and learn how to use it well.

2. **Home equity earns you nothing.** Recognize that your home equity is an asset like any other asset on your balance sheet. Routinely ask yourself if that asset is being used for its highest purpose. Can you use a portion of your home equity to pay off high-interest-rate debt or to purchase an investment property?

3. **In a perfect world, we would all pay cash for everything, but that is not realistic.** Without debt, most people would not start businesses or purchase homes. Understand your credit score and what triggers upward or downward movements.

CHAPTER 4

How Diversification Can Help You

H ere's another financial strategy that may help tip the odds in your favor but goes about it in a different way than the strategies we have discussed previously. Rather than showing the benefits of "when," it shows the benefit of "where." By selecting a broad mix of investments—diversifying—you'll be using another powerful tactic. Compounding and diversification are like teaching chords to a musician or counting to a mathematician. They're the basic building blocks, and all strategies are spin-offs from there.

THE MATH OF GETTING THE MONEY HOME

Diversification isn't a new concept, and it was widely used in the early days of international trade. Just like you shouldn't put all your eggs in one basket, you shouldn't put all your gold on one ship.

Let's say we're back in the 1800s, and you have $10,000 in gold coins buried on a remote island off the coast of Spain. You'd like to get it back to the United States, but there's a problem. FedEx hasn't been invented yet, and government statistics show there's a 50% chance for your ship to get plundered in the pirate-infested waters, and you'll lose everything.

To show the benefits of diversification, we must begin by valuing the money. Is it really worth $10,000? If there's a 50% chance of getting it home, you shouldn't value it as $10,000, but only half that, or $5,000. Multiplying it by the probability to arrive at a value, what's called the *expected value*, makes sense. If there was a 0% chance of getting it home, the money is worthless—no matter how much may be buried. But here, all hope isn't lost, as there's a 50% chance, so your loot should be valued at $5,000. So let's start with the simplest solution to getting your money home—using one ship. If you load $10,000 worth onto one ship and there are no pirate encounters, you'll receive the full amount. However, if you have a fateful crossing, you'll lose it all. There's a 50-50 shot that you'll either end up with $10,000—or nothing at all.

> **A fundamental financial concept that applies to all strategies is to never set yourself up for extreme outcomes.**

A fundamental financial concept that applies to all strategies is to never set yourself up for extreme outcomes. Well, making it all or losing it all is about as extreme as it gets. Further, we valued the cash at $5,000, and by using one ship, it's impossible to get. Is there a way to get $5,000 with a higher degree of confidence?

Yes, and that's where diversification comes in. What happens if you split up your money and load $5,000 on two ships? This is where the math of diversification goes to work. If there's a 50% chance for one ship to get looted, there's only a 25% chance for both ships to meet the same fate. The reason is that if one ship crosses paths with

Blackbeard, it has no bearing on whether the second ship does. It's like flipping a coin. If there's a 50% chance for the coin to land "heads," there's a 25% chance you'll flip "heads" twice in a row. The coin doesn't know what happened on the first flip, so it has no bearing on what happens with the second flip, so the chances of seeing "heads" twice is 50% × 50%, or 25%.

By using two ships, there's now a 25% chance for both ships to survive the trip and for you to receive the full $10,000. Again, this is where people misinterpret diversification. With one ship, you had a 50% chance of getting $10,000, but now it's been cut in half to 25%. What's the benefit of that?

Remember, that's not the idea of diversification. Instead, it's to increase the chances of receiving the $5,000 it's technically worth. Well, with one ship, that was impossible. By using two ships, you have a 50% chance of collecting $5,000, but you still have a 25% chance of getting $10,000. That means there's a 75% chance you'll receive *at least* $5,000. Best of all, the chances for losing it all are cut from 50% to 25% as shown in the chart below:

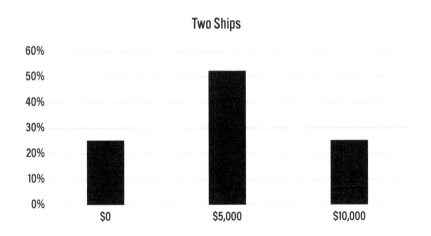

Two Ships

Well, if splitting up the money between two ships works wonders, what are the benefits in dividing it among four ships? Even better. If you divide your money equally among the four ships, you'll have $2,500 loaded on each. The math works the same as it did previously, but now it's just a little more complicated. With four ships, you have a 69% chance of receiving at least $5,000, and a 94% chance to receive at least $2,500—an amount that was impossible to receive by using only two ships. Most important, your chances of losing everything are drastically cut to 6%:

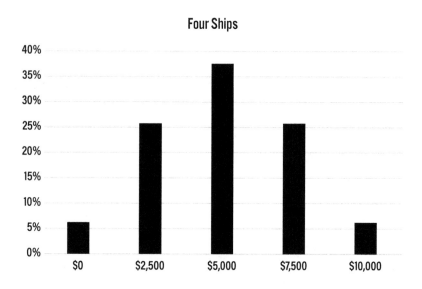

Four Ships

As a recap, remember that you should value your stash as $5,000. By using one ship, you have no chance of collecting that amount. By using two ships, you have a 50% chance, and by using four ships, you've increased the chance to 69% of receiving $5,000. Most important, you've reduced your chance of total loss to just over 6%.

As you increase the number of ships, the probability of receiving *something* increases to near certainty, and the probability of losing it all is reduced toward zero. The simple act of splitting up your money among different ships gives you something for nothing.

Now, go back and revisit the idea shared by those who voice strong opinions against diversification. They are correct that diversification reduces your chances of receiving $10,000. You have a 50% chance with one ship but only a 6% chance with four ships. If you want to maximize your chances for collecting it all, you've got to sail one ship, but just realize it also creates the identical chance for losing it all—and that forces you into extreme outcomes. Diversification, however, greatly increases the chances for receiving the true value of $5,000, and it gives you better chances for receiving at least something for your efforts. Best of all, it reduces your chances for losing it all. Once you've defined your financial goal, it doesn't make sense to put all your eggs into one basket—or coins onto one ship.

INVESTMENT OVERLAP

However, many people, including some financial advisors, often misunderstand diversification. You need to be aware of investment overlap. This occurs when you own multiple investments that appear to be different, but when you look under the hood, you see a lot of similarity. For example, you may own ten mutual funds within your portfolio. On the surface, you feel safer because you spread your money out. Unfortunately, there may be a very large overlap within those different mutual funds. Try not to get distracted by the name of the ETF or mutual fund. Look up the positions and identify the top ten to fifteen holdings. If you see a lot of similar names, you are not as diversified as you think.

GOING TOO FAR

Not only does financial success depend on balance, but so does diversification. Investors sometimes get carried away with the idea, and being overly diversified may be counterproductive—and it can actually cause a drag on your performance. In the previous example, it wouldn't make sense to split your $10,000 value into a million pennies. There comes a time when diversification does its job, and it's not worth carrying the idea out further. Additional costs can begin to weigh on your performance. If you had to pay a small percent for guards on each ship, you'd need to find a balance between the costs of the diversification and the benefits. Investors sometimes will hold one share of every stock in the universe but not realize the costs involved with moving that money into different investments or sectors in the future.

Diversification can also reduce the value of any big performances from some of your stocks. In 2020, the Nasdaq 100 increased over 50% from March to August,[4] mostly led by Apple (AAPL), Microsoft (MSFT), and Google (GOOGL). However, had you held one share of every stock in the universe, those gains would be insignificant. Too little diversification is bad, but too much doesn't make it better. Remember, it's about balance. Just don't forget about diversification.

NUMBER-ONE MISTAKE AMONG EMPLOYEES WITH 401(K) PLANS

Not diversifying is the most common mistake among employees who are offered 401(k) plans or other tax-advantaged retirement accounts. Most of these plans allow you to select broad-based index funds, such as the S&P 500 index, but many also allow you to invest in the employer's stock if it's a publicly traded company. Many people are tempted to invest 100% in their employer's stock. After all, it's the place they've chosen to work, and who'd choose to work for a company they thought was going to fail? However, if you choose to invest all your money into your employer's stock, think about diversification. If your company does well, you'll likely move up the corporate ladder, and earn more money—plus bonuses. But it gets even better: In addition, the stock price will soar, and you'll make even more money. But what if the company suffers, or worse yet, fails?

Not only may you lose your job, but you may even lose most of what you had in the 401(k) plan. Don't think it can't happen— remember Enron.[5] By investing 100% in your company's stock, you're subjecting yourself to extreme outcomes—making it all or losing it all. A basic rule of financial strategies is that, when in doubt, split things up.

It's the very reason why Coca-Cola owns Dasani water, Sprite, Fanta, Minute Maid, Hi-C and Gold Peak Tea. It's why Disney owns Marvel Comics, ABC television, and ESPN. And it's why Proctor and Gamble owns Tide, Gain, Cascade, Febreze, Bounty, Charmin, and Gillette—plus so many more. Splitting investments up works for them, and it'll work for you too.

DIVERSIFICATION OF STRATEGY

Although a lot of attention is given to diversifying the investments you hold, I have found that diversification among strategies can be even more powerful. It is easy to get caught up on small wins and miss the opportunities for better strategies. For example, many advisors and individual investors focus on the same routine financial planning sequence:

- Fund your retirement accounts

- Buy insurance

- Maintain your emergency fund

- Pay down your house

- And maybe open another investment account for excess cash flow

Surprisingly, that is the extent of many financial plans I see. The average financial planning process is plain and leaves people feeling there has to be more to it. Within this routine model, the attention is spent on how much insurance to buy or what mutual fund is better than another. Don't get me wrong. Those are important questions, but I believe financial strategy should be much more creative and dynamic. That is why my team has developed a process that leaves our new clients thinking, *I did not know I could work with an advisor this way*, and *I wish I knew about all of this sooner*.

You do not need to settle for a generic financial plan. Focus on the fundamentals, but don't miss out on the big picture.

Chapter 4 Summary

1. **What really matters is how much money makes it home and how much risk was taken to achieve that.** Diversification can help you increase the odds of a favorable outcome and reduce the odds of a negative outcome.

2. **Investment overlap**: Most investors believe they are more diversified than they truly are. If you own multiple mutual funds, there is a good chance those funds own a lot of the same stocks and bonds. Make sure you are truly diversified.

3. **Overdiversification**: Don't take it too far. If you spread your money out too much, you may not enjoy the growth you are aiming for. Owning fifteen to twenty different stocks is great, but owning three hundred could have an adverse impact.

4. **Strategy diversification**: The success of your financial plan is not about owning mutual fund A, B, or C or stock X, Y, or Z. Finding a mutual fund with a slightly lower internal fee could save you $1,000 per year, but don't ignore the tax strategy that could save you $20,000 per year. I find that too many clients and advisors focus more on products than strategies.

CHAPTER 5

Investing: Putting Your Money to Work

E veryone may not start with the same amount of money, but everyone gets the same number of hours in a day. To get ahead financially, you get one of two choices. First, you can work more hours per day, but eventually you'll hit a limit on how much money you'll be able to make.

Second, rather than working more hours, you can leverage the time you have, and that's done by letting your money work for you. You've earned income by selling your labor and skills, so why not put those dollars to work too? If you have $100,000 invested, it's like having 100,000 employees all chipping in to do more work. Unlike people, they're never late, and they work every minute of the day. That's a big benefit, but don't forget about compounding, which we looked at earlier. Each of those employees produces more employees of their own—interest—which also produces more employees—interest on interest. If you're ever wondered how some people seem to have so much money but not necessarily more skills, it's because they're leveraging their time. They have the same number of hours in a day as you, but they're making better use of that time. That's what investing is all about. But how do you put dollars to work?

Investing is a complex world. There are nearly an infinite number of choices, and each carries its own set of risks, rewards, and fees. If you mention investing, most people assume you're talking about stocks, bonds, mutual funds, or exchange-traded funds (ETFs). Sure, they're great ways to invest; however, they're not the only ways. My firm, Legacy, advises clients on a wide range of investment choices that may never include the traditional stock market. They may choose to invest in myriad ways, such as startup companies, real estate, direct loans, self-directed IRAs, or even start their own business. I have clients who love to research and be involved in the process and others who just want investments that will create dividends and monthly income without having to lift a finger.

In later chapters, I'll open your mind to a fuller spectrum of investing. Some may be perfect solutions for your needs while others may not, but you need to know what's out there in order to avoid "wishing you had known sooner."

Regardless of how you approach putting your money to work, there are two basic ways to approach investing—active and passive. Be sure you understand the differences, because they will dictate the types of investments and strategies you'll use.

ACTIVE VERSUS PASSIVE INVESTORS

Investors can be divided into two basic groups: active versus passive. Active investors do their own research, constantly listen to the news, pick their own stocks, and decide when to buy and sell. The lure is to try to "beat the market," which means they're trying to earn more than the return of the overall market, such as measured by the S&P 500 index. If the S&P 500 increased 10% during the year, active investors are trying to get a higher return by actively timing the market and hoping they know something the market does not. If they can buy when prices are low, sell when high, and get back in at the lows, perhaps they can earn 15%, 20%, 30% or far more because they're so engaged in the process.

Passive investors, on the other hand, do just the opposite. They don't try to beat the market, but instead, just accept the return of the market each year. If the market's up 10%, so be it. They're happy with that. So which is best? It's logical to think that doing a

> It's logical to think that doing a lot of work to time the market will produce superior results, but the math says something far different.

lot of work to time the market will produce superior results, but the math says something far different. In fact, it shows the opposite.

THE MATH OF PASSIVE INVESTING

Passive investing sounds like a lazy couch-potato approach. Nobody wants to say they're not trying with their investments. And who wants to strive for receiving average returns? Well, the math does. Let's say the S&P 500 returns 10% in a given year. What can we expect from the performance of active and passive investors?

There's no question that passive investors will receive the return of the market, so they'll earn 10%. What about the active investors? Can they expect a better performance?

Let's start by dividing the market up between active and passive investors. It doesn't matter which numbers we use, so let's say 70% of investors are passive and 30% are active. However, knowing that the market returned 10%, it immediately tells us the returns of active

WISH I KNEW THAT SOONER

investors: On average, they must also earn 10%—exactly the same amount as passive investors. No matter how unbelievable it seems, the math shows it can't work any other way.

To see why, think back to your college days. Let's say you had a class where 70% of your grade is based on quizzes and 30% is based on exams, and all count the same. At the end of the course, you've earned a 90% average overall. Knowing the overall number, you know you must have also scored 90% on your quizzes and exams. That's the only way your overall average can equal 90%. If you earned more than 90% on your quizzes (or exams), your final average would have been higher. If you scored less, it would have dragged down your final average. Both groups—quizzes and exams—must have scored the same average. So, in our example, active and passive investors earned 10% during the year. Are there any differences between the two groups?

The difference is consistency. Passive investors consistently earn the market returns. They're all doing exactly the same thing, so there's no variation. We know that all passive investors earned 10%, no more, no less.

Active investors, on the other hand, earned the market return—*on average*. That means some may earn more than that in the overall market but only if other active investors earn less. If the market returns 10%, some active investors may earn 15% but only because others underperformed and earned 5%. If one person earns 5% more, another had to earn 5% less. On average, they all earned 10%. Remember, active investors are just trading among themselves, so the only way one can outperform the market is if another underperforms. Active investors, on average, earn the same as passive investors, but with a lot of variation. However, active investors spend a lot more time, effort—and commissions—in an attempt to beat the market. After accounting for these costs, it's doubtful that many find it worthwhile. Even if some do well in a given year, or even over several years, they won't consistently be able to beat the market every year. In the long run, they'll underperform passive investors. To succeed with investing, you must realize an indisputable mathematical fact: You can't beat the averages by doing what the average investor does. The irony is that most investors underperform the market because they actively try to beat it. Later in the chapter, I will show you how to benefit from passive investing by also including *active strategy*.

THE MARKET DOESN'T CARE WHAT YOU THINK

Not only does the math say that active investing is probably more trouble than it's worth, but so does some simple stock market logic. The problem with relying on instincts is that they have nothing to do with a stock's performance. When you go with gut feelings of when prices are high or low, you're only acting on your beliefs. Unfortunately, the market doesn't care what you think. What makes a stock's price rise or fall is determined by what the collective market thinks. It's what everybody else thinks that matters.

The problem with trying to pick the next hot stock is that it's not enough to do your own research. In fact, it's probably the worst thing to do. You'll pay attention to every positive news article, and they'll fuel your conviction that you must be right. All positive news looks like flashing neon lights. But the negative news gets ignored. After all, it must be wrong.

Paying attention to the good news and ignoring bad news is called *confirmation bias*, and it's an easy trap to fall into. The more you're convinced you've found a winning stock, the more you'll invest—and the bigger the risk you're taking. To pick great stocks, you don't need the internet to do research. In fact, that's the worst thing you can do.

Instead, you need a crystal ball to see what everybody else thinks—and those are harder to come by. Once you see investing from everybody else's view, investing changes. You may believe the Sluggish Software Corporation is a dog with fleas. But what if you knew that *everybody else* thinks it's going to be the next Microsoft, and its price will rise from $50 to $1,000 over the next few years? My guess is you'd buy it, even though you don't like the stock.

To make money in the financial markets, you must invest where the money will flow—not necessarily in the companies you like. If you're the only person who believes it should flow into a particular stock, don't expect its price to move. Prices are based on nothing more than perceptions about what the collective market thinks a company is worth. As Gordon Gekko from the movie *Wall Street* said, "Money itself isn't lost or made. It's simply transferred from one perception to another." Even though it's just a line from a movie, it carries a profound message: A company's value isn't determined by the quality of its products, recognition of its brands, or even the amount of its sales. Instead, it's based on what investors think the company will be worth in the future.

The financial markets are "forward looking," which means that investors don't really care what happened in the past. They're only concerned with what's expected to happen in the future. This is exactly why new investors are puzzled after a company announces great earnings, only to see the stock's price fall. Why would the price fall when the earnings were better than expected?

The second that news is announced, it's in the past. Instead, investors look for information about what to expect in the future, and companies provide that shortly after the earnings announcement. The company holds a conference call with analysts and investors and provides guidance about future earnings. If the company says future sales are likely to fall, investors don't care how good the current earnings are. The stock's price will fall despite the great current-earnings report.

What about the reverse? Can it happen? Sure, and that's not uncommon either. A company may release horrible earnings numbers but give positive forward guidance. You may see the stock price rally even though the earnings were bad. To succeed with investing, you must realize it's not what you think that matters. You can't just pick the stocks of companies you think make great products or the ones that have performed well in the past. If investing were only that easy, it wouldn't be investing. It would be an ATM machine.

WHAT ABOUT THE CHARTS?

Active investors often think they can beat the markets because they look at stock charts for clues. Investors who do this are called "chartists" or "technicians," and reading the charts is called *technical analysis*. For instance, they may find that a stock's typical low is $70 while the typical high is $100. Chartists would call the bottom level of $70 the "support" and the upper level of $100 the "resistance" levels. In other words, if the stock price falls to $70, investors are more likely to buy. On the chart, it appears that the prices are hitting a floor, or "support," at that price, and you'll probably see prices begin to rise. On the other hand, if prices reach near $100, investors are inclined to sell, thus making the stock's price appear to hit a ceiling, or "resistance," on the chart. Active investors believe that by buying and selling at these levels it will help them to beat the markets. Sounds logical, but let's look at what the research says. Take a look at the four charts below. Based on the stock prices, which look like ones you'd want to buy? Can you find support and resistance levels or other patterns where you'd feel confident they'll be repeated?

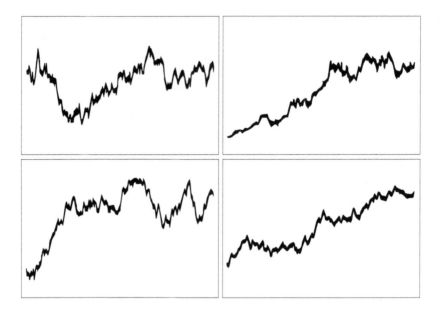

It's hard to tell, right? Now for the surprise. Three of the charts are fakes, created by flipping coins. Each time the coin landed "heads," the stock price rose a dollar, and every time it landed "tails," the stock price lost a dollar. Only one is real, and it's Microsoft (MSFT),[6] which is the upper right chart. Most investors don't realize that stock price charts are based on random price movements. There's no way to predict whether tomorrow's price will be up or down, just as there's no way to predict whether a coin will land "heads" or "tails." Because of that, it's hard to distinguish a real stock chart from a fake, or more convincingly, it's easy to trick the eye with random patterns. People find it surprising that random price changes create such convincing-looking patterns. It looks as if you'd be able to tell when a stock price is "doing well" and will continue to rise versus when it's "about to fall." It seems that way because random prices—and random coin tosses—do create patterns. Sometimes, the patterns are so unbeliev-able that it seems only logical that there must be some other force at work and not just randomness.

If you ask most people, they'd think a random chart means the prices are just going to oscillate sideways back and forth. Instead, you can get long streaks where the chart's moving up and long streaks where it's falling. People are wired to look for patterns, and the eye will see exactly what it wants to see—confirmation bias. If you're determined to find a dog, a fish, or Abraham Lincoln in cloud formations, you're bound to find it.

It is a losing idea in the long run to try to figure out when prices are going to rise or fall by looking at charts or reading the news. You'll be tempted to act, when it's nothing but random noise. Just like a coin landing "heads" five times in a row doesn't make "tails" more likely on the next flip, seeing a stock's price rise or fall consistently gives you little information on what will happen tomorrow. Even if all the fundamentals of the company are picture perfect, there's always the chance for completely unrelated news—such as the September 11 attacks—to change that price path in a split second. If you can't predict tomorrow's news, forget about trying to predict tomorrow's stock price. So if you're new to investing or just don't wish to spend the time, know that passive investing isn't a second-rate approach. You can use it with confidence and let compounding work its magic over time.

> **If you can't predict tomorrow's news, forget about trying to predict tomorrow's stock price.**

SIMPLIFY INVESTING

To make your money work for you, you've got to make investing simple. You need to have a medium- to long-term view. As populations grow and economic activity expands, prices will rise over time. Rather than trying to find the ideal stock at the perfect time, remember that picking one stock—or even a few—isn't good diversification. You're exposing your money to extreme outcomes where you could make it all—or lose it all. Take a look at the bold line in the chart below in July 2018 when Facebook (FB) fell from about $217 to $176, or 20%,[7] in a single day after releasing a quarterly earnings report that fell below expectations. To make it worse, the company announced weak forward guidance, which means the company warned investors that the upcoming earnings would probably also fall below expectations:

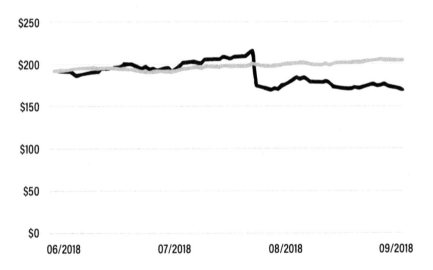

A single day wiped out $120 billion in market capitalization, and the stock continued to slide for months afterward. Facebook may be a great company, but all great companies go through bad spells. There's not a single company that hasn't released bad earnings and seen their stock price plummet. It happens. If you owned Facebook, 20% of your investment was instantly erased. That's the risk you take—and the price you pay—by picking just one stock, or even a few that aren't well diversified. How did your investments perform had you owned the S&P 500 during this time?

Facebook is also in the S&P 500, but because it wasn't the only stock you owned, diversification saved you. The index was flying high through this time, as shown by the gray line, so compounding could continue to work its magic, and your money continued to grow. It's as if Facebook wasn't even in the picture. While it's true that an individual stock may outperform the market, it can just as easily underperform it, in sometimes shockingly big ways. So a big key for making investing easy and successful is to not try to beat the market. Not only does it make things easy, but it puts you in a much better mathematical position. If investing can be made easy by passively investing, why is it so hard for most investors? On one hand, investing is easy: Pick a style and stay with the plan. Emotions, however, get in the way.

EMOTIONS: "MOVE THE FEELINGS"

Whether you choose to be an active or passive investor, investing can be difficult. You may feel you have control over your decisions, but it's doubtful you'll have control over your emotions. The word "emotions" comes from the French to mean "move the feelings," and that's exactly what happens during turbulent times. Markets can go through wild gyrations, and it's difficult to keep emotions in check while your money's melting away.

In 2020 during the COVID-19 pandemic, the S&P 500 index dropped 35% in a little over a month from February to March[8]—but then rallied 60% through August. The trouble for investors is that emotions will nearly choke the life out of you during these precipitous drops. While your rational side may be trying to stick to the plan and buy more shares while prices are on fire-sale discounts, your emotional side will be screaming to sell. And the emotional side usually wins.

Nobody wanted to sit back and watch prices come unraveled, and during COVID-19, it was sometimes over a thousand points down each day. What took years to earn can be evaporated in less time than it took to send the order. Every investor believes it's in his best interest to sell during the panic and buy back later when prices are lower. Unfortunately, everyone thinks the same thing, everyone sells, and everyone is worse off. Welcome to the world of the average investor. That's bad enough, but it gets worse.

Eventually, prices reach such a low point that the "smart money"—big institutions, banks, and hedge funds—jump in to buy. It's this emotional play between fear and greed that causes the "V" bottoms on stock charts, which can easily be seen in the chart below for the S&P 500 index during the COVID-19 pandemic:

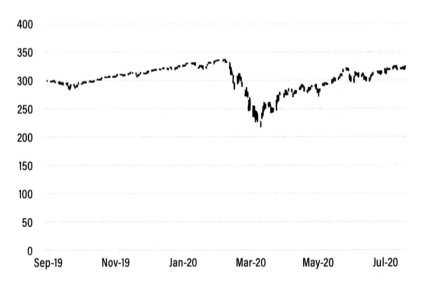

Look at just a few days after the lowest point. The stock prices were nearly straight up for two or three days. Those are usually the big institutions buying. Average investors, however, are nervous about getting into the market so quickly, so they wait—and wait and wait. As more investors begin to buy, prices rise further, causing more to have confidence and buy, which causes prices to rise further. The fall off the cliff is fast and furious because fear is a powerful motivator. The recovery is generally slower. In the business, we say it's the staircase up—and the elevators down.

But take a closer look at the above chart. Had you sold in the middle of the decline, you sold low and bought high—exactly the opposite of what should be done. Think about the destruction: Investors lost 20% to 30% on the way down, but then missed out on the 60% rally. Selling at the first signs of danger sounds like a good idea for preserving wealth but is nothing but a recipe for disaster. In a relatively short time, the market fully recovered, yet many investors had their investment values cut in half after it was over.

My Philosophy

I believe in the market over time but also see opportunities to add value. Whether you wish to be an active or passive investor—or a combination—creative, proactive strategies will separate you from the average investor.

For instance, in 2020, my team felt the market was overvalued in the early part of the year, so we sold off some high-performing equities and bought more bonds. We didn't sell all investments and go to cash or bonds. We just moved away from the extremes and toward the middle. While we did not know COVID-19 was around the corner, the market dropped, and our clients were better protected. After the drop, we rebalanced again by selling bonds that had held their value and repurchased stocks that had declined dramatically during this crisis. As a result, our clients experienced less of a drop while still participating strongly in the recovery. We did not try to time the market, but our strategy rewarded our clients. You don't have to be all in or all out, completely passive or totally active. We believe in low-cost index funds where appropriate but don't believe your investments should sit on the shelf and gather dust when proven strategies can add value.

For traditional stock market investing, whether you're an active or passive investor, you can use constant-dollar or dollar-cost averaging, which we'll look at shortly, to make the random whims of the market work in your favor. The idea is that you'll rarely buy at the low or sell at the high. By using strategies like these, however, you can at least capture the average prices, and that'll put you closer to better purchases and sales.

A VOICE OF REASON

It's not just emotions that makes investing risky. Risk comes in many forms—including advice. That's why you must know the person who's giving the advice. Even if the advice is good, the recommended products may be loaded with fees, not to mention risks.

Consider who's giving the investment advice. Is it someone selling an in-house product? My firm is independent because we don't want conflicts of interest. If it's best for you to invest in real estate, we will help with that. If you want to buy stocks, ETFs, or mutual funds, then we can help with that too. I would never say that advisors from large firms or insurance companies have products that aren't necessary, but it's prudent to have independent advice before you buy a product, especially if it's complex and requires a long-term commitment. That's definitely not the time to wish you had known sooner.

It's important to understand your investments. That doesn't mean you must become an expert, but don't be afraid to ask questions. Be sure you're comfortable with the recommended investment approach.

Don't forget that the investing world can be complex, and there's nothing wrong with saying you don't understand an investment or strategy. Warren Buffett, regarded as the world's most successful investor, never bought shares of Enron because he didn't understand how they made money. And we all know that story ended as one of the largest bankruptcies in US history. Apparently, Enron wasn't quite sure how it made money.

For some clients, I may recommend high-risk, complicated strategies that may thrive. However, that same strategy for other investors could be a disaster if they're not going to stay the course.

Yes, the investment world is complicated, but that doesn't mean that complicated investments are better. As long as you're putting your money to work and using sound financial principles, you're investing. This is another reason why it's so important to have a financial advisor who can be the voice of reason during emotional times. Financial markets go through ups and downs, but when they fall, history has shown that they tend to recover over time. The better strategy is to buy on these dips—or terrifying drops—and let the long-term economy put things back together. However, if you're on your own, whether actively or passively investing, emotions will get in the way. A good financial advisor will help you stick with the plan as well as provide long-term strategies to help you bolster returns that you probably wouldn't be able to capture on your own. Remember, investing means putting money to work for you. Having the money but not the discipline isn't investing. It's gambling.

Chapter 5 Summary

1. **Passive investing is not boring investing.** A lot of data supports the benefits of removing emotion from the process and allowing the market to work for you. This does not mean you have to buy a few investments and let them gather dust on the shelf. There is a balance between passive investing coupled with creative strategies.

2. **The stock market is very good at responding to information before you are able to.** Avoid chasing market trends that can cause people to buy investments after they have reached their peak. As a result, they miss the upside while still participating in the downside.

3. **I believe markets are efficient, and there is a place for passive, low-cost investing.** However, I have learned that proactive strategies and portfolio rebalancing may tip the odds in the investor's favor and lead to better results.

I meet with clients weekly who wish they would have had our team review their investment portfolio sooner; they didn't know what they didn't know. Don't risk paying too much in fees or taxes for another day. Reach out to my team for help.

InvestLegacy.com

CHAPTER 6

The Big Money Is in the Waiting: Solving the Dilemma of When to Buy or Sell

I t's when you sell that counts. That's a common piece of advice offered by most financial professionals. In other words, it's not so much when you buy that matters. History has shown that stock markets typically trend upward, so even if you are unlucky enough to buy near a market top, if you have the patience to wait, there is a good chance a new high will be reached in the future. The trick, according to them, is when you sell. If you can sell near market tops, you can reinvest at lower prices and get the compounding force to work even harder.

It may sound like a good idea, but if you're going to reinvest near market lows, the buy side matters too. If it's a benefit to buy shares at $100 and sell at $105, there must be an equal benefit in selling at $105 and buying back at $100. Both decisions matter.

If you've read this far, you already know that stock price changes are random, so a goal of selling near a top and buying near a bottom makes about as much sense as trying to guess coin flips. You'll get some right, you'll get some wrong, and you'll have mediocre results overall. There are things you can do to improve your results.

As I've already mentioned, strategies are what matter. While you may not be able to consistently guess which direction prices are headed, there are strategies that make great use of that uncertainty.

STRATEGY #1: TAKE A LONG-TERM VIEW

As populations grow, demands rise, and productivity increases, businesses expand and sell more stuff, and that ultimately pushes prices higher. It takes time. In the short run, however, anything can happen. Earnings reports, world events, political risks, and other news can always send prices higher—or lower. Anything goes in the short run, and that's the problem with trying to increase your wealth by buying and selling over short periods of time. Sure, you may buy low and sell high, but you're just as likely to buy high and sell low. Information arrives randomly in the market, and you never know what each day brings. However, history has shown us that there is an upward trend in the stock market over time.

The next chart is for Home Depot (HD), considered to be one of the best managed companies on Wall Street. From 2000 to early 2020, there's an obvious long-term upward bias, but there are also significant dips along the way.[9] Even with the precipitous drop from COVID-19 at the right side of the chart, the company nearly fully recovered within three months. On February 20, 2020, it fell from $247.02 to a low of $140.63 on March 18. In just 27 days, the company lost

43% of its value. Yet, by May 18, it had risen to $245.35, thus nearly fully recovering in just 88 days:

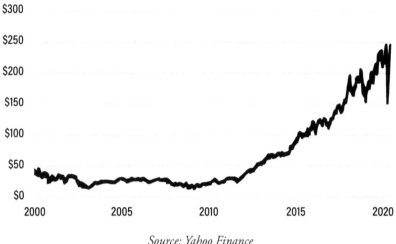

Source: Yahoo Finance

This chart proves the long-term upward drift of this stock. What is debatable is what defines the long run. It's certainly not over a few months, or even a couple of years, as many investors think. Stock prices can vary wildly in the short run. A long-term view keeps you centered. It keeps you from having false expectations that prices only rise. With the proper perspective, you won't panic and sell at the lows. You need to develop the mindset that, for wealth generation, it's the long run that matters.

Charlie Munger, vice chairman of Berkshire Hathaway, summed it up like this: "The big money is not in the buying and selling—but in the waiting." So a simple but powerful strategy is to understand that prices fluctuate, sometimes greatly, over time. Don't worry about it. If you're a short-term speculator, sure, it can

> With the proper perspective, you won't panic and sell at the lows. You need to develop the mindset that, for wealth generation, it's the long run that matters.

be a problem. But if you're taking a long-term view and investing for the long run, these short-run fluctuations simply don't matter. With a long-term view, you'll see market downturns for what they really are—buying opportunities.

Even with a long-term view, it's still best to use a broad-based index to get the benefits of diversification. And don't try to find the ideal stock at the perfect time because you already know what you've read here—that picking one stock or even a few isn't good diversification. You're exposing your money to extreme outcomes, and those are always best to avoid. But take your choice. If you have the skills and confidence to select your own stocks, you can do so. If not, use the S&P 500 index. Regardless of your answer, a simple strategy is to take a long-term view and not worry about the fluctuations that simply don't matter in the long run. The only problem, as I've said before, is that expectations can get overpowered by emotions. If you decide to choose your own stocks, be sure you have the emotional control to weather the storms.

STRATEGY #2: DOLLAR-COST AVERAGING

Once you've committed to investing money for the long run, how do you keep your emotions from getting the best of you? When do you make your first—and subsequent—investments? When do you sell? They're all good questions, but remember, it's not when you buy or sell that matters. It's strategies that count.

Investors are always trying to buy when prices are low. As discussed earlier, the low points are nothing you'll ever know about until after the fact, and that's what makes the decision impossible to say for sure. Low prices can always move lower. However, you'll probably never buy at the lowest price, perhaps not even close, so it's an unrealistic expectation. On the previous Home Depot chart, the lowest price is represented by one tiny speck sitting among thousands of prices over the 20-year period. Out of all prices that will occur over the years, the day you pick to buy probably won't be the one. It doesn't make sense to think you have a reasonable chance of beating such great odds, so it's best to leave emotions—and predictions—out of the equation. But how?

That's where *dollar-cost averaging* comes to the rescue. It's a simple yet powerful tool that anyone can use. Just invest a fixed amount of money at set times, say $100 per week, $500 per month, or $1,000 each quarter. The amounts and time frames are up to you. But you'll usually make these purchases into mutual funds because they allow you to buy fractional shares so that 100% of your investment goes to work. However, you could certainly use stocks, indexes, ETFs, or other assets.

As market prices fluctuate, you'll buy some shares at low prices and others at high prices. While you'll never get lucky enough to buy all shares at the low, you'll also never be unlucky enough to buy them all at the high. The periodic purchases reduce the potentially wide range of prices you'd otherwise face. Because you're investing the same dollar amount each time, you'll buy fewer shares when prices are high, but you'll buy more shares when they're cheap. In other words, dollar-cost averaging creates diversification among your purchase prices, and that's why it helps to temper the volatility. For example, let's say you're investing $1,000 per month into a mutual fund. Over the next six months, the fund's prices are $100, $120, $80, $60, $70, and then back to $100. You've invested $6,000 total and acquired 71.8 shares for an average price of $83.57:

MONTH	INVESTMENT	PRICE	SHARES PURCHASED
1	$1,000	$100	10
2	$1,000	$120	8.3
3	$1,000	$80	12.5
4	$1,000	$60	16.7
5	$1,000	$70	14.3
6	$1,000	$100	10
	Total = $6,000		Total = 71.8 shares

What's the benefit? Notice that while prices fluctuated wildly, the fund's price was $100 in the first month and the sixth month. Had you purchased all your shares in the first month, you just broke even after six months. It was a lot of time and effort for nothing.

By dollar-cost averaging, however, you spent a total of $6,000 and acquired 71.8 shares for an average price of $83.57. With the stock at $100, you're up nearly 20%. Notice the price fell from a high of $120 to a low of $60. That's a 50% swing during the six-month period, which is highly unlikely, and yet it didn't matter. You still came out with a nice gain. To see why it works, take a look at the following chart. It's a computer simulation over a 24-month period where the stock price randomly fluctuates between $100 and $150, which is shown by the gray line. The black line, however, shows your average price during the two-year period:

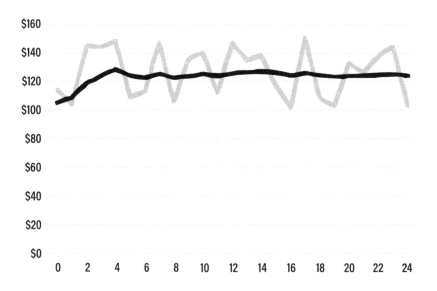

Despite the large fluctuations in prices, your average price is relatively stable and never too far from the current price. On the other hand, had you purchased all the shares at one time, there's a good chance it could be near a high price, and when prices fell to the lows, you'd panic and sell. Dollar-cost averaging makes long-term investing easy, as it takes all guesswork out of your decisions, yet gives a high probability for success.

DRAWBACKS OF THIS STRATEGY

All strategies have pros and cons, and depending on your assumptions, one may be better than another for you. Dollar-cost averaging is a great tool for investors who get nervous over market drops, and who panic and sell at the lows. The best scenario for dollar-cost averaging is for prices to drop while you're building the position, but then rise back to the initial purchase price, as shown in the previous example. In those cases, your average price will be below the current market price, and that's why the example resulted in a gain even though the price started and ended at $100. Lots of price volatility, lots of emotions, and yet you ended up with a profit. That's a nice benefit.

However, that doesn't mean that's how it'll always turn out. If you continue using dollar-cost averaging over long periods of time, and prices drift higher, your average cost will be higher than it would have been had you purchased all your shares at once. You'll still make money, just not as much had you invested it all in the beginning. If you have a large amount of money to invest today, it's mathematically best to dump it all in today, ride through the ups and downs, and let compounding work its magic over the long run. But if you think your emotions may get the best of you, consider dollar-cost averaging.

It's also a great strategy for people who may not have a large chunk of money today to invest but want to create a large portfolio over time. This is often how people build IRAs or 401(k) plans.

The worst scenario for dollar-cost averaging is for prices to continually fall. That's a rarity but could certainly happen with an individual stock. For those times, your average cost will be above the current market price, and you'll definitely end up with a loss. However, the loss won't be as big as if you bought the shares all at once, so while it's not much of a consolation, dollar-cost averaging would at least reduce the size of the loss. Stock market prices can get exceptionally volatile. Even if they've been relatively calm in the recent past, it's no guarantee they're going to stay that way. That's why it's called risk. If you think the roller coaster rides of the stock market will force you to sell, or if you've had trouble holding through declining prices in the past, dollar-cost averaging may be the one simple strategy you need for financial success. You don't need to worry about the right time to buy. You don't need to worry about fluctuating prices. Just worry about making sure you get started.

STRATEGY #3: CONSTANT-DOLLAR AVERAGING

If you're looking for shorter-term investments, there's a similar sounding strategy called *constant-dollar averaging*. However, for it to work, you must have a sizable amount of money today that you're willing to invest. With constant-dollar, take the total amount you're looking to invest over time and put the *average of that amount* into the market today. For instance, in the previous example, we assumed stock prices fluctuated between $100 and $150 over a twenty-four-month period. If you were planning to invest $1,000 per month for those two years, you could, instead, take the average, which would be about $12,000. In other words, by investing $1,000 per month for twenty-four months, you'd have invested $24,000 total. The halfway point would be about $12,000. (Technically, it would be $12,500, but as long as you're close to the average, it's good enough.)

Start by putting $12,000 into the investment today. Next, pick a fixed time interval where you'll measure the performance, perhaps every month or quarter. The more volatility you expect, the shorter the time periods you'll want to use. You'll check your value at each time period and rebalance back to your starting level. For instance, let's say you invest $12,000 and will rebalance every month. After the first month, the value of your investment has risen to $13,000. The goal is to keep it at the initial $12,000 value, so you'd sell $1,000 worth of the investment. After the second month, let's say it has fallen to $11,500. Buy $500 worth to bring it back up to $12,000. Each month, you're either buying or selling to maintain the initial $12,000 value. What's the benefit?

By keeping your investment at a constant level of $12,000, the strategy forces you to buy low and sell high, a perfect recipe for success. The strategy works beautifully for short-term investments where there's a lot of price volatility. As long as prices fluctuate in ranges and don't continually rise—or continually fall—you'll increase the value of your holdings by buying low and selling high.

THE DRAWBACKS

The strategy works beautifully as long as prices go back and forth with no real direction. However, if prices continually rise, you'll only sell each month, and that means you'll eventually run out of shares. On the other hand, if prices only fall, you'll continually buy and run through your cash. Constant-dollar averaging is a great tool for short-term investing where there's a lot of expected volatility.

However, that doesn't mean it can only be used for short-term trading. It can also be a wonderful strategy for investors who wish to supplement longer-term investments. For instance, perhaps you had long-term investments you were holding through the COVID-19 pandemic. However, you also wanted to take advantage of some of the oversold conditions. This could be a good time to take some additional cash to supplement the long-term position for the next few months.

KEEP IT SIMPLE

No matter which strategy you decide to use, it's best to keep it simple. With today's advanced markets, it's easy to complicate things. You have stocks, bonds, mutual funds, ETFs, ETNs, REITs, limited partnerships, futures, forex, options, swaps—and that's just starting the list. You have levered funds and inverse funds. If that's not complicated enough, there are hundreds of funds within mutual funds, ETFs, and ETNs. You can find funds for anything you can think of, including truly obscure niches like livestock, fight against obesity, trends among millennials, social media, video games, and artificial intelligence. There's even a flight-to-quality fund to capitalize on money flowing to the United

States during times of panic. If there's a need, you can bet there's a fund. Unfortunately, the diverse menu confuses investors, so they often feel it's best to take a small piece of everything. That's overdiversification, and it just makes things complicated, not to mention expensive. Even if you're an experienced investor, it's best to keep things simple. Even legendary billionaire investors like Warren Buffett and John Bogle advocate simple investing by sticking with the S&P 500 index. It gives you all the diversification you could need, and because it's passively managed, the expense ratios are among the lowest of any funds. There's no reason to not get started, and there's no reason to make it complicated. Complicated doesn't always mean better.

When investors chase returns, they're simply trying to find stocks with the "fastest" returns, so it's the pursuit of profits that means it's usually not worth switching. When driving in rush-hour traffic, the best strategy is to pick a lane—and stay put. Sometimes it'll move slower, and other times it'll move faster, but if you spend your time frantically switching, you're taking a lot of risk, and you're not going to get home one minute sooner. Whether you're driving or investing, it's never a good idea to take more risk but get nothing in return.

That's how it goes for investing. Pick a broad-based diversified basket of stocks, such as the S&P 500, dollar-cost average, and stay put. If you also own individual stocks whose prices have fallen, hang tight. Other investors will realize they're the ones which are likely to see better future gains—the faster lanes—and start to switch. The thing to understand is that stock prices ebb and flow over time based on information. Sometimes the information is bad, and other times it's good. If you can't predict the information, you can't predict the selections, at least not consistently. Sure, sometimes you could get lucky, but sound investing isn't based on luck. Instead, understand that when all investors are trying to do the same thing—find the best performing stocks—it's best to play the averages and stay put. It doesn't pay to switch.

STRATEGY #4: CHEAP DOESN'T MEAN BETTER

Buy low, sell high is a common mantra among investors. Unfortunately, they mistake that to mean buy "cheap," and it's why people are attracted to penny stocks or other inexpensive investments. They believe that if they can buy cheap investments, they can buy a lot of shares, and the more shares they own, the more they make for each dollar rise. For instance, let's say the Frugal Fund costs $1 per share and the Lavishly Luxurious Fund costs $100 per share. A $10,000 investment in Frugal nets you ten thousand shares while the same investment would only gain 100 Lavish shares. It seems like you're better off with ten thousand shares because every dollar move in the fund creates a $10,000 gain—much better than the $100 you'll get by buying Lavish shares. The logic sounds good until you realize that stock prices move in percentages. If both companies perform equally well, their prices will move the same percentages. Let's say both increase by 10% so Frugal is trading for $1.10 and Lavish is $110 at the end of the year. Regardless of which one you bought, your investment has also increased 10% to $11,000. The number of shares has nothing to do with your performance. Scanning a long list of funds to find the cheapest ones isn't a good idea. Instead, you should focus on which fund will likely perform better, not which one allows you to buy the most shares. In fact, you'll often find identical funds trading at different prices at different companies. For example, the Schwab S&P 500 Index Fund (SWPPX) was trading for $41.62 in March 2020, while shares of the Vanguard 500 Index Fund (VFINX) were selling for $250.10 at the same time. Both track the S&P 500 index, so the cost of the fund simply doesn't matter. In cases where two funds track identical indexes, you should check the expense ratios. Schwab charges 0.02% while Vanguard charges 0.14%—seven times as much. Now the choice becomes clear, and between these two, SWPPX is the better choice, not because the shares are cheaper but because of the lower expense ratio. If both funds charged identical expense ratios, it wouldn't make a bit of difference which one you pick. Don't shop for investments based on the cost. Cheap doesn't mean better, because the number of shares you own has nothing to do with the results. Instead, ask yourself which investment is likely to perform better. If the cheaper investment is expected to perform better, that may be a good reason for buying. But it's never a good idea to buy it just because it's cheap.

STRATEGY #5: HAVE A PLAN, STICK TO IT, MAKE ADJUSTMENTS WHEN NEEDED

Once you've created an investment plan, stay with it. That's probably the most important point. Investing is easy when everything is going right. It's easy to put more money in the market when prices are rising. The hard part is staying with the plan when things go wrong. That'll rattle your nerves, challenge your emotions, and make you question your judgment. Switching isn't the answer. If you're holding a well-diversified basket of stocks, such as the S&P 500 index, don't dump your investments and try to switch to individual stocks that are doing well. Lower prices mean you'll buy more shares, which lowers your average cost. To make the most of your investments, you want to accumulate a lot of shares at low prices. When markets are down, it's an opportunity to buy—not a time to panic. Setting up an automatic investment plan is a great way to ensure it gets done. It's seamless, and if you're truly committed to the plan, your budget will quickly adjust. Always remember that investing is for your benefit. You may have to deal with periodic pressure, but you'll also keep all the gains, provided you stay 100% committed.

Now that we've covered investing essentials, let's take a look at some of the products you may be using to meet your investment objectives.

Chapter 6 Summary

1. **The longer you are invested, the impact of the exact day you invest becomes less important.** You have the ability to reap rewards by just staying in the game. A lot of investments pay capital gains and dividends just because you own shares. You want the investment to grow as well, but that is not the only way you can make money.

2. **Millionaires are not made overnight.** Your financial success will be a culmination of many wise decisions and your commitment to them. Try to avoid the "get-rich-quick" mindset.

3. **Dollar-cost averaging:** Buying into investments at a routine frequency can help you reduce the risk of buying in on a bad day. Try investing monthly so you know you will be buying in when the market is up and when it is down. Trying to time a market dip before you buy in can cause you to sit on the sidelines for years.

CHAPTER 7

Annuities: Problem Solvers or Financial Problems?

Annuities are some of the most popular investments, yet they can be confusing for investors. The idea behind annuities is actually pretty simple, but the dozens of variations and conditions make them complicated. Unfortunately, they're also among the products that can carry the highest commissions, so they're a popular playground for high-commission salespeople and the primary reason some annuities have gotten a bad reputation. However, none of these characteristics—complexity or high commissions—means annuities are bad. When structured correctly, they can be powerful solutions to many financial problems.

Like all financial products, annuities are tools. If you need a hammer, a screwdriver is going to look awful. That's unfortunately why some annuities have gotten bad raps. People end up buying them as answers to the wrong questions. However, if they were always bad for everyone, they wouldn't exist. The high commissions attached to some don't necessarily mean they're overpriced. As you'll find out, annuities can provide guaranteed monthly streams of income for life, and that can be expensive to create and insure. These added costs make them expensive and therefore difficult to sell, so higher commissions are attached for the additional work required by salespeople. No matter what the product may be, as long as there's competition, high fees are more often signs of high costs—not rip offs. Most of the time, investors who feel they got stuck with a bad deal got lost in the details and bought something they didn't need or understand. My business is an independent financial advisory firm, not an annuities sales firm. So I'm not here to put you into an annuity unless it's exactly what you need.

If you speak to an insurance firm, you'll hear all the positives of annuities. If you talk to most other financial firms, you'll hear the negatives. I take a middle-of-the-road approach. I realize that annuities, like all financial products, were designed to solve problems. If it's a great solution that provides the missing piece to a difficult puzzle, it's hard to argue it wasn't a good deal. The best thing to do is arm yourself with information before deciding. For now, forget everything you've heard about annuities and approach this chapter with an open mind. You may find perfect solutions. Instead, if you think you'd never need one, that's good information too. It's better than buying one and wishing you had known sooner.

ANNUITIES DEFINED

At the most basic level, an annuity is a steady stream of cash, paid at fixed intervals, over a period of time. For instance, a mortgage is an annuity. It's the same payment made each month. Car loans, boat loans, and student loans are other types of annuities. You could even create your own annuity by making steady deposits each month or quarter to a savings account. Keep this basic point in mind, because it's the common thread for all annuities.

FINANCIAL ANNUITIES

When you hear about annuities in the financial markets, they're talking about any number of financial contracts where you *receive* a continued stream of income, usually a fixed amount, over a given time. The word "annuity" comes from the French word *annuité*, which is derived from the word *annual* because many of the original annuities were paid annually. Today, most are paid monthly, but you can get them paid monthly or quarterly. For those who get lucky enough to win the lottery, one of the choices most states offer is to receive a steady stream of payments, say $1 million each year for twenty years. That's an annuity. With the lottery, you win these payments, but with a financial annuity, you buy them. Would you like to have a steady $1,000, $5,000, or $10,000 per month during retirement? You can buy an annuity that guarantees these payments for as long as you live. Not sounding so bad now, right?

All annuities offer some type of guarantee. It may be a rate of return, such as 5% per year, a guarantee against loss of principal, or a guarantee of income. Most of the time, people are looking for guaranteed income, but you should understand that many types of annuities exist that can solve other complex financial problems.

While you may be able to buy annuities from many types of brokers or agents, only insurance companies, sometimes called the *issuers* or *carriers*, issue annuities. While there are hundreds of issuers, the bigger names like MetLife, Prudential, and the Hartford account for about 95% of all annuities sold each year. Annuities are issued by insurance companies because they're part insurance and part invest-ment. They act as an investment because you may get more back in return. They're part insurance because you're also paying for an insurance policy that guarantees a rate of return or monthly payments. An entire world of annuities exists, and no matter how creative you get with thinking of a financial problem, an annuity, or combination of them, can probably solve the problem. Annuities may even be solutions to financial problems you never knew existed.

Annuities can be broken down into two categories: *immediate annuities* and *deferred annuities*.

IMMEDIATE ANNUITIES: I WANT MONEY NOW

Immediate annuities are the insurance company's answer to pension funds. Most companies don't offer pensions, so chances are, you're working for one of them. However, you may have saved quite a bit through 401(k) plans or IRAs. The trouble is you must manage that money to outpace inflation and hope that you don't outlive your nest egg.

Another big risk is that you could experience a market crash like we had in 2007–2008, when the market dropped 50%. Even during the last quarter of 2018, the market dropped 20%. When dramatic drops like this happen, do-it-yourself investors often panic, sell at the lows, and buy back later at the highs. The result is that a chunk of their money vanishes, and needless to say, that can permanently alter plans for the worse. This is called a *sequence of returns risk*. In other words, losing 20% of your portfolio when you're thirty years old isn't the same as losing it when you're retired. The timings, or sequences, of these gains and losses matter.

For instance, if you had $300,000 invested in the market in October 2018 but sold at the lows in December, your account fell to $240,000: that means $60,000 went up in smoke in three short months. The sad part is that one month later, the market gained 15%,[10] and it fully recovered by mid-April. For investors who panicked, however, the money is gone for good. Even if they bought back during the recovery, they now own fewer shares, so any dividend income is reduced. It's one thing if you experience market downturns during your working years because you have time to buy at the lows, and you can ride out the recovery. During retirement, however, rather than buying more shares, you're withdrawing money to meet expenses. These market uncertainties are what make immediate annuities attractive for some people. But how do immediate annuities work?

Immediate annuities usually require a single lump-sum payment today and are consequently called a single premium immediate annuity (SPIA). In return, you'll receive monthly income beginning within a timeframe of your choice, which can range from within the year to next month.

Like any financial transaction, the cost depends on how much you're looking to receive along with a number of other factors such as age, gender, and interest rates. Because your investment will earn interest, the higher the interest rates, the higher your monthly payments will be. These contracts come in two basic forms: First, you can buy one that'll pay as long as you live, which is called a *life annuity*. Second, you can choose for it to pay for a fixed amount of time, say ten or twenty years—whether you're alive or not.

For example, in 2019, a sixty-five-year-old man could pay $100,000 and receive about $525 per month for life. Women usually receive a bit less, perhaps $475, as their life expectancy is longer, so the payments are lower. By purchasing an annuity, you're taking cash today and "annuitizing" it over a long period of time. It's like you're creating your own pension fund. But will it pay off?

GETTING YOUR MONEY BACK

There's a calculation you can do to find how long it takes to get your money back, which is called the *breakeven point*. If you receive $525 per month, that's $6,300 per year. By investing $100,000 for those cash flows, you'd break even after $100,000 ÷ $6,300, or nearly sixteen years. So, if you're sixty-five today but live until eighty-one, you'd just break even. If you live past eighty-one, the annuity paid off, while it was a loss for the insurance company. That's the risk side you're trying to avoid but the insurance company is accepting. However, if you die early, the insurance company keeps the money (although there are some annuity contracts that can pass the balance to your estate). That's the insurance company's compensation, along with other fees, for accepting the risk of having to make far more payments than expected.

The chart below shows the number of dollars gained or lost for each year alive. For instance, if someone pays $100,000 and dies in the first year, $100,000 is lost. After sixteen years, there's no gain or loss, so the investment just breaks even. However, for each year survived above sixteen years, the investment begins to pay off. The longer the life, the better the annuity pays off:

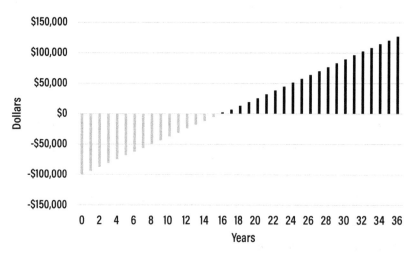

Chart created by author.

It's the idea of possibly dying sooner than expected and "wasting" the investment that turns many people away from annuities. That misses the entire point of insurance. Avoiding annuities for fear of not getting your money's worth isn't good financial planning. Always remember that annuities aren't purchased for capital appreciation. Instead, they're risk-management products. If you're concerned about irregular cash flows, market crashes, or outliving your money, annuities solve the problem because you're guaranteed to receive the same amount of money every single month—always.

Note that many variable annuities have the chance to grow, and if they do, your monthly payment could go up, but it will not go down. There is also a difference between taking monthly guaranteed payments that leave a death benefit for beneficiaries or annuitizing the contract, which gives up any remaining benefit and turns it into a true annuity. Most clients never annuitize their contracts. They just take guaranteed payments for their lifetime (unless the contract goes to zero, at which point they have to annuitize).

Annuities provide another benefit. By being part of a bigger risk pool, you're diversifying risk. In a similar way, diversification showed how splitting your money up among more ships reduced the chances for a bigger payoff, but it also increased the chances of receiving the average. That's exactly the idea behind annuities. If you know the monthly annuity check is something that'll help to meet your goals with 100% certainty, it's hard to argue that it's a bad deal. In exchange for that guarantee and peace of mind, you must accept the risk of dying sooner than expected and having your money go to others. It's the pooling of these risks that allows the insurance company to create annuities in the first place. It's not a risk. It's a benefit.

IMMEDIATE ANNUITIES FOR COUPLES

Another common choice for married couples is to buy annuities that'll pay during your life plus another's, which is called a *joint and survivor annuity*. If a husband or wife wants to receive payments as long as one is alive, the monthly payments will drop, say from $525 to $450 per month. The reason is that the chance for both to die is less than for either one individually, and the insurance company therefore expects to pay out over a longer time. Immediate annuities are great ways for people to turn a large sum of money into a steady stream of income that cannot be outlived. Maybe you just sold your business, received a big bonus or inheritance, or are about to retire and cash in your 401(k) plan. No matter what happens to the market or any future investment decisions you make, you know for sure you'll receive that income. Once you commit to the annuity though, you won't have access to the cash for emergencies—or anything else—without paying a big penalty to the insurance company, usually 10% or more. Be sure it's money you can live without.

THE RISK POOL BENEFIT

You may be wondering if it wouldn't be better to invest the money yourself in a risk-free investment and create your own annuity. While you could do it, there are two big risks.

First, you have a risk of falling interest rates. To see why, let's say you have $100,000 to invest in a risk-free investment such as Treasury bills (T-bills). If interest rates are 5%, you'd earn $5,000 per year, or effectively $416 per month. I say "effectively" because T-bills pay semiannually, or every six months, so you're not actually going to receive a check each month. That, however, isn't the risk. If interest rates remain the same, you'd always have that same monthly income—and you'd have the $100,000 to pass to your heirs. However, if interest rates fall, the income you'll receive will fall too. That leads to the second risk.

If you wanted to maintain the same monthly income, you'd need to tap into the $100,000 principal. If interest rates continue to fall—like they did from 2007 to 2016—you'd need to take more and more each year from your principal, and that means you may burn through your $100,000 long before you expected. Naturally, if interest rates rise, it's a bonus, so that's nothing to fear. However, both of these risks are eliminated by purchasing an annuity, and you'll be guaranteed that same monthly payout for life.

The insurance company can make the guarantees because you're part of a much bigger risk pool. Insurance companies have about a bazillion dollars in these contracts, and some people will live longer than average, and some won't. Remember, however, that if you die sooner than average, you generally don't receive any money back. Instead, the insurance company uses this excess money, called *mortality credits*, to continue paying for those who do live longer than average.

You don't get that benefit when you do it yourself, and that means you run a bigger risk of outliving your money. When you invest on your own, you're just dealing with principal plus interest. However, when you receive your monthly check from an annuity, part of it is principal, part is interest, and part is from mortality credits. Mortality credits are a key reason why annuities will generally outperform investors doing it on their own.

Now it should be easy to see the risk of creating your own annuity. If you invest $100,000 into a T-bill and earn 1.75%, you'd effectively receive $145 per month. But if you wanted to receive $525 per month, you couldn't invest the entire $100,000. Instead, you'd have to set some of that $100,000 aside to make up the monthly shortfall, say $5,000, and invest the $95,000 balance. If you do this each year, your principal is dwindling, and you're also faced with falling interest rate risk. That means you've got a much bigger risk of outliving your money. Annuities eliminate that risk.

COMPARING RATES OF RETURN

Risk pooling creates another benefit because insurance companies can offer higher interest rates than you could get on your own. Part of the reason is that the companies are investing much larger pools of money, so they get better rates. Second, depending on how the mortality credits are balancing, more money may be paid out.

However, unless you understand how annuities work, the interest rates can be deceptive. For instance, in late 2019, a one-year Treasury bill was paying 1.75%, which means a $100,000 investment would earn $1,750 per year, or effectively $145 per month. At that same time, an immediate annuity for a 65-year-old man was paying about $525 per month. It appears that the annuity is paying a much higher interest rate. If you can earn $525 per month, it adds up to $6,300 per year, which is implying a 6.3% return. However, there's a big difference between investing in T-bills and annuities. When you invest in T-bills, your monthly income is solely generated from the principal, or $100,000 in this example. No matter how long you stay invested in T-bills, you could always receive your $100,000 back in the future. That's not true for annuities.

Instead, when you receive your monthly annuity checks, you're receiving some interest, but you're also receiving part of your principal back, and that's why the interest rate appears much higher. For example, if you give me $100,000, and I pay you $25,000 per year for four years and nothing else, you shouldn't think you earned 25% on your money. I simply returned your principal back to you over four years. Remember, however, that annuities aren't about capital appreciation. They're risk-management tools, so don't get too caught up in comparing interest rates. But if you do, be sure you're comparing apples to apples—interest to interest—and not interest to principal.

DEFERRED ANNUITIES: LET'S WAIT A WHILE

The second main category of annuities is the *deferred annuity*. As the name suggests, you're deferring the time before receiving monthly payments, say ten or twenty years. With an immediate annuity, you pay a lump sum today and receive immediate monthly income. With deferred annuities, you're paying monthly premiums for years before you'll ever receive monthly income.

Deferred annuities are the insurance industry's solution to a savings account, and they account for about 80% of all annuities. While you're contributing money, it's called the *accumulation phase*, and issuers allow you to pay a single lump sum, monthly premiums, or a combination of the two. For instance, you could pay $20,000 today, but also pay $100 per month.

Some issuers allow flexible premiums where you can make payments whenever you'd like and in any amount you choose. It can be a good solution if you're a long way from retirement because it doesn't lock you into steady premiums if an emergency arises. However, it also creates an easy escape hatch that allows you to quit making payments simply because you can. Regardless of which choice you make, during the accumulation phase, your money earns a small guaranteed rate, which depends on the current interest rates. In 2019, you could expect about 3% per year.

Deferred annuities can remain in the accumulation phase indefinitely, but they always grow tax deferred. That means you don't owe taxes on the money until you begin receiving income. Even better, there's no limit on how much you can put into a deferred annuity, which makes them great planning tools for the wealthy.

At maturity of the contract, you have several choices of getting your money back, which is called the *payout phase*. First, you can get a check of your accumulated savings and be done. In this case, the annuity provided a long-term guaranteed return. Second, you can convert your money into an annuity. However, if you convert it into an annuity from the same issuer, the monthly income you'll receive will usually be less than if you shopped the markets. So, most people will take the accumulated money and simply buy an immediate annuity that's offering better payouts. Regardless of your choices, the basic idea is that you pay into the annuity for years, which allows you to build a larger savings. After that, you can choose to turn it into a monthly income stream.

EMERGENCY ACCESS

No matter how much planning you do, you can never plan for emergencies. If you must access your cash, you can generally do so in the first several years. It's also possible to completely surrender the contract and receive its current value, less any surrender fees—but the penalties are steep. A typical charge is 7%, but they can run as high as 20%. However, it's usually a sliding scale, so each year that goes by, the percentage usually falls by one percentage point until there are no more fees. The IRS may also impose a 10% penalty if you withdraw funds before age 59½, so make sure you can hang in for the long term with deferred annuities. If you need to access the money, be sure it's for an emergency, not because you need a down payment on a Lexus.

It's also possible to purchase annuities in individual retirement accounts (IRAs) and Keogh accounts, which are retirement plans for self-employed people. However, it's usually not a good idea to do that because these accounts are also tax deferred. The only exception may be if you're sitting on a large amount of cash and about to retire. You may decide to use some of your money to buy an immediate annuity to provide income for life. While annuities can be a great deal and an important part of retirement planning, you should max out your retirement accounts, such as IRAs or other tax-deferred accounts, first. Annuities have higher costs than retirement savings plans, so you want to get the most valuable money to work first. Remember to put money where it's treated best. Once those obligations are met, consider annuities.

VARIABLE ANNUITIES: UNDERSTAND THE FEES

If you've ever heard about variable annuities, you probably heard they're dogs with fleas. As stated earlier, that doesn't necessarily mean they're bad. It just means you need to be sure of all the terms of the agreement. Like any financial product, for the right problem, it may be the perfect answer.

When you buy immediate or deferred annuities, your money goes into a general account, which means it's pooled with others. That's why the issuers can get higher rates of return and offer higher guarantees to the buyers. It's also why some of the mortality credits get divvied up among all annuity buyers. However, if you buy a variable annuity, your money goes into a single account—yours—and it's invested into broad-based market investments, similar to what you may have done with 401(k) plans. Your money grows according to the overall markets, which gives you the possibility of increasing your money through capital appreciation in the stock market. It also gives more room for losses. Your account values change, or vary, with market conditions. Your monthly payments during the payout phase depend largely on how your investments performed in the stock market. Variable annuities are therefore like a mutual fund tied to an insurance policy.

INSURING THE INSURANCE

Insurance companies are in the business of selling insurance, so it's no surprise that you can get nearly anything, including annuities, insured. Most variable annuities can be purchased with a death benefit rider, which is just a supplemental policy guaranteeing certain minimums to your heirs. If you invest $100,000 into a variable annuity, and the market value is less when you die, your beneficiary gets the $100,000 value. Some issuers offer step-up benefits, which means this guaranteed value gets increased each year by a certain amount. Another interesting rider values your annuity each year on the contract's anniversary based on the highest value during the year. If you invested $100,000, but your investments had a high value of $130,000 during the year, then that becomes the payout to your beneficiary if you die. That value is a high-water mark, so it can never decrease, but it may increase if the market value rises further. While riders sound like a great idea, the more insurance, and the more complex the riders, the bigger the fees. Don't insure things just because you can. Instead, make sure it's a fee you're willing to pay to reduce a risk you don't want.

UNCOVERING THE FEES

Regardless of the apparent benefits, variable annuities are not recommended by most financial advisors for a variety of reasons. Probably the biggest drawbacks are the associated fees. These commissions are typically not paid up front but instead are built into the annuity, so you will need to do a little digging. You'll have a surrender fee for terminating the contract within a certain time, usually six to eight years. There are also mortality and expense charges, averaging 1.25%

per year, to compensate the insurance company for certain risks. Finally, there are administrative fees, which can run another 3% per year. That's a lot of fees, and they can more than double the cost to construct the same portfolios yourself in the market. Even bigger fees, though, are the taxes. Generally, if an investment is held less than one year, it's taxed as ordinary income, which could be as high as 37%. But if you hold an investment for more than one year, you get favorable tax treatment and pay long-term capital gains, which is anywhere from 0% to 15% for most people. Only the highest income bracket pays 20%. The government rewards you for holding investments more than one year.

That's not how taxes work with annuities though. Any capital gains are taxed as ordinary income according to your income bracket at the time of distribution. No matter how long you've held the annuity, you're subjected to unfavorable short-term tax rates. This can tack on another 10% to 20% in expenses. Variable annuities are not necessarily all bad, and there are times they make financial sense. One of the more common uses is for asset protection. About 75% of US states protect variable annuities from creditors. Other forms of retirement savings, including IRAs, are easier to access by creditors through the courts. For those in high income brackets, or those vulnerable to lawsuits, variable annuities may be a good way to protect some of your assets. For retirement planning though, variable annuities are probably a last resort. There are better ways to accomplish the same thing for less.

QUESTIONS BEFORE BUYING

Annuities can be great tools for financial planning, especially retirement. This chapter just touched on fixed and deferred annuities, but there are many variations and insurance riders that can be tailored to

WISH I KNEW THAT SOONER

perfectly meet your needs. Understanding that annuities exist and that they may be a great solution to your financial needs is a step in the right direction. You can always say no, but you can't say yes once it's too late. However, before you consider an annuity, there are some questions to consider. It's also best to consult with a trusted financial advisor, because you may not know the right questions to ask.

Ask about the Fees

Annuity guarantees come with a price. If you want a guaranteed return, it won't be much. If you want guaranteed streams of income for life, there'll be costs. No matter how good an annuity may sound, always ask about the fees. Fees are often hidden in the rates of return. If the issuer promises to pay 3%, it sounds like it's only a gain to you, but that's because you don't see how much was deducted to arrive at that number. There are also early surrender, administrative, transfer, and distribution fees, but there's another big one. Annuities, like mutual funds, charge annual expense ratios, which deducts a percentage of total assets—not your profits. A 3% fee is common, so if your annuity earns 10%, you're receiving only 7%. The relatively "small" fee reduced your returns by 30%. Generally, the more complex the annuity, the higher the fees. This is one of the reasons variable annuities carry higher fees than immediate or deferred annuities. If you decide on an annuity, try to keep it as simple as possible with as few riders as possible.

Ask How You Can Get Your Money Out

Putting your money into an annuity is easy. It's amazing how quickly the issuer will cash your check. Getting your money out, however, can be a different story. This doesn't mean that annuities are fraudulent. Instead, remember that the issuer is investing that money and distributing it to others. If everyone demands their money back at the same time, it destroys the very benefit the annuity is trying to create. Many types of financial products, including hedge funds and mutual funds, have early redemption fees for the same reason. For annuities, however, the fees can get really big. Be sure to ask about the rules for getting your money out should you need to. If you can't, be sure it's money you can live without before signing the contract.

Investigate the Strength of the Issuer

Most annuities are issued by only the strongest of insurers, but that doesn't mean their products aren't infallible or that an insurer hasn't faced lawsuits for underhanded dealings. With today's online world, it's not hard to do a quick search to get reviews of any issuer you may be considering. Also, be sure to check with the Better Business Bureau, state's attorney, and state insurance commissioner for any reviews or bulletins of pending lawsuits. If you're dealing with the top-name firms, there's little to worry about, but it never hurts to take a few minutes to see what others think. You're going to be paying into the annuity for a while, so be sure it's a company you'll like.

Research the Tax Implications

Annuities may solve problems, but once you consider taxes, they may create more problems than they solve. For instance, most assets left to heirs receive a step-up basis upon death, which means the cost basis is valued at the time of death and not the amount originally paid. If you paid $400,000 for your home and sell it for $1 million, you'd pay taxes on the $600,000 capital gain. But if you leave the home to heirs, their cost basis is "stepped up" to the current million-dollar market value. They could sell the home, collect a million dollars, and pay zero taxes. The step-up provision is one of the most powerful ways to keep assets in the family—and to avoid taxes. However, if your heirs receive $1 million from an annuity, they owe taxes on it, no matter what kind of annuity it is. One problem is that your heirs may be in a lower tax bracket, say 15% or 25%, but get launched into the highest bracket when they receive the annuity. Be sure you speak to a financial or tax advisor if part of your concern is leaving a gift for your heirs. They may receive a lot less than you think, and that gift may cost a lot more than you realize.

Ask How the Annuity Will Solve Your Problem

Annuities will always sound like the perfect solution to all the world's problems when you're listening to a sales pitch. However, be sure to ask yourself which problem it's going to solve for you. If you can't pinpoint the problem, it's probably not for you. If you're willing to take more risk, you may be better off leaving your money in the stock market, using a blend of stocks and bonds, or combining these along with an annuity. Because there are so many possibilities, it's always best to consult with a financial advisor—a fiduciary—before buying. You may find a better solution for less money. For some questions, however, you may find that annuities are the perfect answer.

Remember, there is always a trade-off. If you have an investment with lower risk, you will most likely have lower returns. If you have an investment with more "guarantees," there is a good chance your fees will be much higher.

Annuities tend to be more popular in times of economic uncertainty. People can be attracted to investment options that have "guarantees" or "protection" of some kind. Remember, there is always a trade-off. If you have an investment with lower risk, you will most likely have lower returns. If you have an investment with more "guarantees," there is a good chance your fees will be much higher.

Have a Strategy

Here's a great example of a strategy-focused plan instead of a product-focused plan.

I remember a couple, we will call them the Millers, I met with around 2009. The country was still recovering from the real estate and stock market crash, and the pain of that was still fresh on people's minds. The Millers had saved well and did not live an extravagant lifestyle. They wanted their money to grow but were also afraid of running out of money at some point. As a result of market turmoil and their own fear, they invested most of their retirement funds into a variable annuity. They liked the idea of monthly guaranteed income, so they jumped in headfirst. What they didn't understand at the time is that if they needed more income than what was guaranteed on a monthly basis, they would be penalized for taking that withdrawal. So, they lost liquidity, which is an important part of any retirement plan. In addition, we showed them that they were paying over 3.5% per year in fees for the "protection." On top of that, their investments within the annuity had dramatically underperformed a diversified market portfolio which lost them another 4%. Let's do the math together.

This couple had invested $1 million into an annuity and were receiving $4,166 per month of income. Their 3.5% of fees per year equaled $35,000, and the lost performance cost them another $40,000. In this example, the peace of mind and security they received from the annuity came with a $75,000 price tag. Ouch. This was hard for them to hear, and just as bad, there would be a 5%, or $50,000 surrender fee to unwind the annuity.

So how would my team have approached this situation?

We go into initial client meetings with no personal agenda. Our only goal is success of the plan, regardless of what products are used. We would have discovered that the Millers need around $4,000 per month to cover their bills. This does not include "fun" spending, but we know their biggest concern is running out of money to pay their bills. Their fear does not come from not being able to take nice vacations; they want to have fun in retirement, but they know those expenses are not a need. Their ultimate goal would be to have total monthly income of $6,000 to pay bills, donate to charity, and have fun.

Their joint Social Security is around $2,000 per month. So, to cover their bills, we need only another $2,000 per month from a safe source. The same annuity they purchased will pay them a 5% annual income. If we work the math backward, we know they would need to deposit $480,000 into the annuity to generate $2,000 per month.

This would leave them with $520,000 to invest to generate the other $2,000 per month they want. They are not free to invest in low-cost, liquid investments. While the annuity funds would still have higher fees and be less available, most of their money now has low fees and no restrictions to access. Assuming the fees in their new investments was around 1.2% per year, this strategy change will save them close to $120,000 in fees over ten years. That is a big deal!

In the next chapter, we're going to look at one of the most misunderstood investments of all and one that could be one of the most profitable.

Chapter 7 Summary

1. **Try to remove preconceived notions that annuities are all good or all bad.** They are unique tools that can be used at the right time to solve specific problems.

2. **There are many types of annuities that can be used to accomplish different goals.** Learn the difference between fixed, variable, indexed, immediate, and deferred.

3. **Fees are an issue in the absence of value.** Annuities can have very high fees, and you need to know that before you are potentially locked into one. Some people are comfortable paying a higher fee if that means a company takes on the market risk and guarantees a monthly check for a lifetime. Avoid paying higher fees if you do not plan on using the benefits you are paying for.

4. **Know what questions to ask before investing in an annuity.** Many annuities lock you in for a long period and charge surrender fees to get out. Avoid the feeling of being trapped and wishing you knew more sooner.

CHAPTER 8

Real Estate Investing: Subject to Inspection

Real estate cannot be lost or stolen, nor can it be carried away.
Purchased with common sense, paid for in full, and managed with
reasonable care, it is about the safest investment in the world.
—FRANKLIN ROOSEVELT

R eal estate is a great investment. Unfortunately, I have seen a lot of people lured into the world of real estate investing without understanding the necessary strategies, potential pitfalls, and expenses. As a result, when they crunch the numbers, they often make a worse rate of return than a passive stock or ETF that required little to no effort on their part.

The key takeaway from the above quote from Franklin Roosevelt is that real estate is a great investment if you know what you are doing.

Real estate has a unique property in that it's the key ingredient to nearly all productivity. Whether it's a small doughnut shop, large shopping mall, expensive office complex, or enormous farm, it begins with real estate. Even in today's online world, computer servers and storages don't live in the "clouds." They need a place to sit. Real estate is the solution.

As populations grow and technology develops, people's needs change, which leads to better ideas. Real estate eventually gets pushed to higher uses, and that means the price must eventually rise. It may take time, but it's bound to happen. Take a look in your city. You may see a small diner torn down and a McDonald's built in its place. Fifty years ago, the diner was big enough to serve the locals breakfast, lunch, and dinner. Today, it's not. Eventually, somebody realizes the land isn't producing what it's capable of. There's "missing money," so it would be advantageous to buy it and put something else in its place to solve the problem. That's the basis of capitalism: Who can find the best use for a resource to solve a problem?

If you can find the best use of a resource to solve a problem, you'll be rewarded with profits, but some people may misinterpret what that means. They think profits are the result of greedy capitalists moving in and charging higher prices. But with a little thought, you should see that profits simply reflect the moving of resources to a better use. The land was capable of producing that value, but the diner that occupied it simply wasn't able to do it. If the land has the ability, someone will eventually figure out how to do it. The problem is that you can't move on top of the diner, beside it, or under it. There's only so much land, so that also means the diner's value just went up to reflect the missing money. You don't need to have the ideas that generate profits, but you do need the land.

That's right. Over the long haul, real estate is a fairly safe bet, and returns have held steady through decades. Since 1960, there's only been one bad decade, the 1990s, but even then, returns were basically flat. You may not have made money, but you certainly didn't lose much. We've certainly seen worse from other investments at times. However, not only can real estate produce great returns over the long run, but it can also be used to create profits today.

PRODUCTIVITY IS THE KEY

They key to making money in real estate isn't necessarily just about buying, holding, and selling. In addition, you can also put it to use today. You can build apartments and receive rents, you can plant seeds and sell food, and you can build shopping malls and receive lease payments. You can put property to work in many ways, so while it's appreciating over time, you can collect money today. Now, before you panic, I'm not suggesting you buy an apartment complex or a John Deere tractor and start planting corn. Later in this chapter, I'll show how easy it is to invest in real estate and have others do the management for you. But first, you must understand that productive assets are a key to creating wealth, so any investment professional who advises against real estate is either not forward thinking—or has something else to sell.

> You can put property to work in many ways, so while it's appreciating over time, you can collect money today.

Productive assets are the key to generating wealth, and that's why billionaire investor Warren Buffett has never been a fan of buying gold. In his words, it's not "procreative." That is, gold will never produce more gold or anything else for that matter. An ounce of gold is just an ounce of gold, and that's all it will ever be. Gold is a nonproductive asset, which means the only way you can profit from it is in hopes that someone else pays more for it in the future, which is sometimes called the "greater fool theory." In other words, you'll only profit if there's someone else—a greater fool than you—willing to pay a higher price. If gold is $1,500 per ounce, the only reason for buying it is that you think the price will be higher in the future. There's no way to actually measure a "true" or "intrinsic" value. Instead, today's value is only based on expectations of what people think others will pay in the future.

Real estate is productive, and that makes it different. For this reason, you can't depreciate land for tax purposes because it's assumed to have an unlimited useful life. A small dumpy piece of land may not appear that attractive, but that doesn't mean it's not worth much. If a McDonald's could be built that would earn $100,000 per month, the land is worth a lot. Years later, if an office could be built that would earn $1 million per month, it's worth a lot more. That's when you'll see the McDonald's come down—and a new office complex go up. Again, it's not necessarily worth a lot because there's some sort of inherent value in the property, such as sitting on gold or oil, but *because of what the property can produce.* So, real estate has the ability to get profits from two angles. First, you can gain price appreciation over time. Second, you can earn investment income today. With both of these benefits, many investment experts still say "no" to real estate.

THE TWO EDGES OF FINANCIAL LEVERAGE

As with all investing, there are good and bad approaches. For most people, their real estate holdings consist of one investment—the home they own. They may have put a small amount of money down and completed the deal with a big mortgage. The property, however, doesn't produce anything. There are no rents or incomes of any kind, but there are a lot of expenses. So if they are to "invest" in real estate, they think it means they must buy another house and hang on for decades. They scrimp and save for another down payment and leverage themselves to the hilt. That's probably a dangerous way to approach it, but it's not because the property's value isn't expected to rise over time. Instead, it's because of the leverage that comes with it.

Let's take a look at what that word means. In the world of physics, a lever is a tool that allows you to create a big force by exerting a smaller force. If you've ever had to change a flat tire, a car jack gave great leverage because you could lift a two-thousand-pound car with little effort. Financial leverage works the same way. It means that small change in the asset's price, say 1%, generates a greater percentage of profit, perhaps 10%. Financial leverage is always created with borrowed money. For instance, let's say you buy a $200,000 home but put $20,000 down and borrow the remaining $180,000. At this point, your investment, is the $20,000 you've deposited, which is your *equity*, and you can think of it as "what you own" minus "what you owe." Here, you "own" a $200,000 home but "owe" $180,000, so your equity is the remaining $20,000.

If the home's value rises 10% to $220,000, your equity increases to $40,000. That's because you could sell the home for $220,000 and pay off the $180,000 mortgage, which leaves $40,000. Because you put $20,000 down and walked away with $40,000, you doubled your money. So, a 10% increase in price created a 100% increase in potential profits.

That's financial leverage at work. You paid only 10% of the purchase price, but you get to keep 100% of all future price appreciation, less the $180,000 owed to the bank. Your leverage is therefore 100% ÷ 10%, or 10-fold. You can think of this as a 10x magnifying glass. If the property rises 10%, you'd therefore earn 10 times that, or 100% on your money. If the property had instead risen 20%, you'd earn 200%, and so on. The less you put down, the bigger the leverage, and the bigger the returns. Leverage is one of the appealing features of real estate, but it's also a double-edged sword, and it cuts both ways. It can magnify gains, but it also magnifies losses. If the property's value decreases by just 5%, your equity falls by 10 times that, or 50%. If it falls by 10%, you'd lose 100% of your equity. Any decline greater than 10% puts you under water, which means you owe the bank more money than the home is worth. During the 2008 financial panic, home prices in many areas declined by 30% or more. If that happened, your $200,000 home would be worth $140,000, which would leave you with a $40,000 loss, or 300%—exactly 10 times the 30% drop. So the danger of real estate isn't necessarily that property ownership is inherently risky. It's the leverage.

The risk is that you may need to sell quickly. If the real estate market is taking a nosedive, it's also likely that the overall economy is heading into a recession. You could get laid off and not be able to afford the monthly payments. If you're forced to sell at the low, you'll learn about the risk of financial leverage the hard way. Because real estate is so expensive, it's almost done with borrowed money—a lot of it—and that means there's a tremendous amount of leverage. That's the danger, and it's the reason Roosevelt was careful to include, "purchased in full" in the opening quote. So, the real benefit of real estate ownership is the ability to produce cash while holding the property. The cash can cover the mortgage and put additional money in your pocket while you sit back and hope the property appreciates. Again, this doesn't mean you need to buy rental properties, and I'll show you how to get all the benefits without actually buying property. But for those who do have the cash, it's much easier today than it was just ten or twenty years ago.

Savvy investors can use online tools to search for properties, find valuations, and economic analyses, which show income levels, shopping, schools, and other information about the area. You can even use Google Maps for free satellite images of the properties and surrounding areas, so there's no need to drive all day looking at properties. And while you're online, you can even quickly apply for a mortgage. The process is much simpler than when you had to spend six months with a real estate agent searching for homes. Also, online sales services have put dramatic downward pressure on commission rates. It used to be a nonnegotiable 7% rate, which would usually be split by the buyer's and seller's agents. Today, real estate agents are in heated competition for sales, so for every agent who says no, there'll be one who's willing to say yes. Don't be afraid to negotiate.

TAX BENEFITS OF REAL ESTATE

A big benefit of real estate is that investors can not only get monthly income or value appreciation, but they also get invaluable deductions. First, you can depreciate, or recover, certain costs associated with putting a property into service. Remember, you can't depreciate land, but you can depreciate most things sitting on it, which is what I'm referring to when I say "property." The reason is that the property is assumed to be losing value due to normal wear and tear. Of course, it may appear that most properties appreciate over time, but it's usually because of the land. Changes in supply and demand can certainly raise property values, even in the short run. However, if a house sits on the land long enough, eventually it'll be worthless. Whether the house or rental unit may be appreciating, you can still get tax deductions today.

As a general rule, you can not only depreciate the costs of the property, but also any costs with getting it up and running. For instance, maybe you must get certain licenses, hire cleaning crews, pay for repairs, and other costs associated with getting the property ready to rent. You can also depreciate *capital improvements*, which are structural or restorations to enhance the property's value, prolong its life, or adapt it to new uses.

Depreciation is called a "noncash deduction," sometimes called a "phantom" expense, which means you're not directly writing a check to pay for any losses with the property's declining value. Instead, you just get a nice tax break because of the depreciating property value—even though the value may not actually be falling. This puts real estate in a category all its own, and you could end up with monthly cash flow, but still show a tax loss. The result is that you get to lower your tax liabilities and potentially save thousands of dollars per year in taxes. It may sound too good to be true, but you must understand that the government creates incentives like this so people will create housing, and other businesses that help to solve day-to-day problems. The government can't solve them all, so it creates incentives for others to do it. The deductions aren't tax loopholes or underhanded tactics. They're simply incentives—and if you're willing to do the work, the incentives will work for you. Depreciation is just the beginning of the benefits.

You'll usually be able to deduct property tax, insurance, and mortgage interest too. If you hire a management firm to take care of rentals, you can deduct management fees and advertising costs too.

You may also choose to turn your real estate investing into a business by starting a corporation or LLC. That'll open the doors for even more deductions including accounting, legal, and continuing education fees. You could deduct office space, including a home office. Anything used to run your operation counts, too, such as computer, printer, internet, PO box, and phone. Travel expenses and car mileage can be deducted too.

For larger purchases, Section 179 of the IRS rules can be used. It allows you to expense a long-term asset as if it is short term. Whether the equipment is new or used, it still qualifies.

For 2020, you're allowed to deduct up to $1,040,000 under Section 179 and deduct the full amount in the year purchased, on one condition: It must be put in use during the same year. This can be a life saver for taxpayers. For example, assume it's 2020, and you're planning to spend $5,000 for surveillance equipment for an investment property. However, you find your tax bill for 2020 is $2,000 more than expected. You can buy the equipment in 2020—even if it's December 31—and put it in use to get the full deduction the same year. If you're in the 28% bracket and pay 15.3% self-employment tax, you're reducing your tax bill by about 28% + 15.3% = 43.3% of the $5,000 cost, or about $2,165. By purchasing the equipment in the current year and expensing it under Section 179, you have no taxes due, and you have the equipment you were going to buy anyway.

So, why not make all deductions under Section 179? It seems like a good idea, but if you're starting a business, it's likely you'll have losses, so expensing the entire amount isn't going to be a benefit. In these cases, it's better to use ordinary depreciation methods so that you'll likely have income to offset.

CAPITAL GAINS

Capital gains are another benefit of real estate. For most assets, you'll pay capital gains tax on the profits. If you buy a house for $200,000 and sell it for $300,000, you'll owe tax on the $100,000 gain. How much you owe depends on how long you held the investment. Remember, if those are realized within one year, it's called a short-term capital gain, and you'll be taxed based on your income bracket. For 2020, the highest bracket is 37%, which would subject you to $37,000 in taxes. However, if you hold for at least one year plus a day, the investment qualifies as a long-term capital gain. For 2020, that could be as low as 0% or a maximum of 20%. Real estate, by its nature, is usually going to be long term. Even if you buy a home for speculative quick flip, by the time you close, repair, and renovate, a year will quickly pass. Even if you're lucky enough to renovate a house in under a year, it could take several months to sell it. On the other hand, it's easy to sell stocks or other electronically held investments just because the market looks shaky, or just because you're looking for quick cash. Investors often do, and inadvertently subject themselves to higher taxes. Real estate almost forces you to be a long-term investor. It may take you longer, but Uncle Sam will get less, and that means you'll earn more.

SAVE ON TAXES: THE 1031 EXCHANGE

Section 1031 of the IRS code provides another advantage for real estate investors. It's called a 1031 exchange, and it can be one of the strongest ways to save on taxes—and even pass assets to heirs tax-free.

A 1031 exchange allows investors to do a "like-kind" exchange, which means you're just swapping one asset for another similar one. In the eyes of the law, if the seller receives no money, there is no capital gain. So a 1031 exchange effectively allows you to transform one investment into another without triggering a capital gains tax.

The original like-kind exchange rule goes back to The United States Revenue Act of 1921, which allowed for investors to exchange securities and *non-like-kind* property that did not have a "readily realized market value." However, in 1967, T. J. Starker challenged the IRS and convinced the court that if two *like-kind* properties were swapped, no taxes should be due either. As a result, you'll sometimes hear 1031 exchanges called a Starker exchange. Since then, the idea has been incorporated into IRS rules.

The law initially spoke of "investment property," which was

intended to mean real estate. However, some people interpreted it to mean other collectibles such as art or classic cars, so it created a loophole for investors. The 1031 exchange has widely been used to swap nearly any asset, including art, collectibles, precious metals, royalties, franchise fees, intellectual property, and digital assets such as cryptocurrencies. However, that changed in 2018 when the Tax Cut and Jobs Act (TCJA) said it was now only available for qualified real estate, but not personal property.

Here's how the 1031 exchange works.

First of all, it's best to use an administrator to handle the swap to be sure it conforms to all the details of the law. You don't want to just say you swapped it out as a 1031 exchange and not expect the IRS to have questions. You can usually find a flat-fee administrator for under $500.

There are two main reasons why you should have an administrator. First, you're not allowed to "touch" the money, which means if you hold, or in any way control, the proceeds, the exchange is disallowed. Second, it's difficult to imagine that the property you're interested in buying is owned by someone who just happens to want a property you own. Therefore, you're most likely going to sell your property first but then need some time to either find the replacement property or get the deal consummated. You'll usually have 45 days to identify a replacement property and 180 days to complete the deals. Because of the expected delay between selling and buying, the administrator can hold the proceeds in escrow to show that no cash actually exchanged hands.

Of course, there are other rules, and it's another good reason for using an administrator. Generally, the exchange must be for the same taxpayer. The IRS views the exchange as though you're still continuing to hold the property, just in a different form, so the name must be the same on the purchased and sold properties. The property must be located in the United States, as well as the property you'd like to buy. However, if you own foreign property, you can use a 1031 exchange, provided it is exchanged for another foreign property.

The property must also be for investment purposes, so you can't exchange a rental property for a home you're going to live in. But you can swap land, office buildings, warehouses, and rental properties. However, you must be careful that the IRS doesn't consider it as "stock in trade," which means it's inventory that's held as part of your normal course of business. For instance, you can't be a developer and "exchange" the homes tax free. You also can't buy properties with the intention of flipping for quick profits.

The purchased property's value must be equal to or greater than the one you'd like to exchange. If the replacement property is less, the difference is called "boot," and you'll owe taxes on the boot in the same tax year. The reason is that the 1031 exchange assumes you're transferring the full value and not trying to grab tax-free equity. If you don't transfer the full value, you'll owe taxes on that difference. However, 1031 exchanges don't get you off the hook entirely from paying taxes. Instead, they just allow you to defer them. Eventually, you'll most likely cash out at some time and owe taxes then.

For instance, let's say you paid $200,000 for a property that's now worth $900,000. You find a new property worth one million dollars. By using a 1031 exchange, you could pay the $100,000 difference but owe no taxes on the sale. Your new cost basis is $300,000. Notice that if you sold the new property for the current million-dollar value, you'd owe taxes on the $600,000 difference—just as if you didn't use a 1031 exchange. Let's look at the advantage with deferring the tax far into the future.

You're paying taxes with cheaper and cheaper dollars. For

instance, if you cash out of this new property in twenty years, the 3% inflation rate will whittle the tax bill down to an effective cost of $332,000—almost half. If you held for thirty years, the effective tax is $247,000—nearly 60% less. However, there's no limit on the number of times you can use a 1031 exchange, so you could continue to increase the value of your holdings while continuing to defer the tax. But here's where it gets even better. The 1031 exchange could allow you to keep assets in the family and never, ever pay one cent in taxes.

If you hold the properties until death, you can pass them to your heirs, who get a "step up" basis, which means their cost basis is the current market value. If they sell the properties at that time, all capital gains taxes are avoided. *It's one of the best-kept secrets at keeping money in the family, and it can only be done with real estate.*

QUALIFIED OPPORTUNITY ZONES

Real estate can not only benefit you as an investor, but it can also benefit you if others invest. Prior to TCJA, the 1031 exchange was a great way to defer taxes. Remember, it used to be used for nearly any kind of "investment" property. However, nearly all of those advantages have now been cut. But there was a silver lining. The TCJA had a hidden gift that some experts are calling the greatest tax shelter in American history. That's a big claim. So what's all the commotion about?

By using this gem, you can sharply reduce, even eliminate, capital gains, and it's done through Qualified Opportunity Zones, or QOZs.

A group called the Economic Innovation Group had been lobbying the government to create incentives for investors to rebuild high-poverty, low-income areas. The group was led by American entrepreneur Sean Parker, who cofounded the file-sharing computer service Napster and served as the first president of Facebook. Apparently, he had the pull, and the idea of QOZs was born. Here's how they work: The IRS allowed the governors of each state, possessions, and territories to designate by March 21, 2018, up to 25% of certain high-poverty, low-income areas as a Qualified Opportunity Zone. Once named, they retain their designation for ten years, until December 31, 2028.

Investors can now invest the deferred gain of nearly any investment—not just real estate—including intellectual property, cryptocurrencies, patents, precious metals, machinery, royalties, franchise licenses, artwork, collectibles, fleets of autos or trucks, aircraft, marine vessels, broadcast spectrums. Even racehorses and professional player contracts count. How do you invest in a QOZ?

It's actually quite easy, because you don't have to own the property. Instead, you must invest through a Qualified Opportunity Fund (QOF), which is a business set up for the sole purpose of pooling investments into a QOZ. Think of QOFs like a mutual fund that anyone can invest in. These businesses can invest directly in a property located in a QOZ. They can also choose to invest in a QOZ business, provided it derives at least half of its income by owning or leasing a property in a QOZ. You don't need to live or work in one of these zones to capture the tax benefits. You only need to invest in a QOF. It doesn't get any easier.

The idea is that you can invest the *capital gains* from a sale or exchange to an unrelated party into a QOF within 180 days. Unlike a 1031 exchange, you can also choose to invest a portion of the gains. The capital gain is triggered on the date you choose to sell, or at the latest, on December 31, 2028, when all zones lose their status. The realized gain is the lesser of the deferred gain or the fair market value in the QOF on that date. In other words, if the QOF's value dramatically increases, you'll just owe the taxes on the original, smaller deferred gain. But if the QOF flops, you'll only owe the taxes on fair market value of the fund, which could be a lot less than the original taxes owed. However, you don't have to wait until 2028 to get tax benefits. After five years, 10% of the originally deferred gain is forgiven. After seven years, 15% is forgiven. But if you hold for at least ten years, you'll completely eliminate the gain on the appreciation in the QOZ fund, which means you'll get tax deferral today and tax-free gains in the future. How good of a deal could this be?

Let's say you recently sold a property in 2020 for $1 million with an $800,000 capital gain, but you invest the full million dollars within 180 days into a QOF. For tax year 2020, you won't pay capital gains on the sale because the money got invested in a QOF. In five years, in 2025, your $800,000 gain will be reduced by 10% to $720,000. In two more years, in 2027, you'll reduce the gain by 15% to $680,000. At that time, your QOF investment's cost basis is stepped up from zero to $1 million. In 2030, you'll realize the million-dollar gain on the sale of the QOF, but none of it will be taxed because it was held for more than ten years. Even better, there's no cap on gains, so the bigger the capital gains, the bigger the savings. A $10 million gain held for just five years would save $1 million in taxes.

Qualified Opportunity Zones emphasize the importance of understanding the newest financial innovations, tax laws, and strategies. As economic needs change, so do tax laws, but keeping up is a full-time job. It's one of the most important reasons for working with a financial advisor. Imagine if you sold a $10 million property and didn't know about QOFs—which the tax shelter experts are calling the greatest in American history. That's potentially $1 million you gave up, and if you're trying to make money, you can't afford to lose millions.

MAGNIFYING YOUR REAL ESTATE GAINS

Real estate offers another hidden advantage, and it's a key reason why it plays such an integral part in building the fortunes of the super wealthy. How can investing in real estate be that much different from investing in something else, say a mutual fund?

Most investments earn a return on the money you have invested. If you put $200,000 into a mutual fund that earns 6% per year, it's increasing by $12,000 per year. However, if you withdrew half the money, it would only earn $6,000 per year. The amount of money you earn is directly tied to the amount you have invested, which is sometimes called a *direct-recognition* asset. But real estate is different.

Rather than having $200,000 invested in a mutual fund, let's say it's sitting as equity in your home. If the home appreciates 6%, how much did your equity earn? Did you guess the same $12,000 as for the mutual fund? It sounds logical, but the answer is that you can't be sure by just knowing the equity. The reason is your home's equity earns nothing—not one single penny. To answer the question, we need to know the home's value, not the amount of your equity.

For instance, if it's a $500,000 home, a 6% increase represents a $30,000 gain, but for a $1,000,000 home, it's a $60,000 gain. A $2,000,000 home would earn $120,000. You get the idea. Your investment's return depends solely on the value of the home. It has nothing to do with your equity. This is known as a non-direct-recognition investment. A non-direct-recognition asset will appreciate even if you take some of the equity out of the asset. A $500,000 home will still appreciate at the same 6% even if you take out a home equity line of credit of $200,000 on the house. Well, if your equity's sitting there doing nothing, there are some interesting strategies you can use to put it to work—and get tax deductions to boot. For instance, if you have equity in your home, you could refinance and put it to work. Sure, you'll add to the mortgage, but you'll free up a large amount of money that can be used for another purpose, such as paying off high-interest-rate debt, making improvements to the property, or accomplishing other goals. If the bank will charge you 4% to lend you the money and you can put that money to work earning more than 4%, the math will be in your favor. There will most likely be fees charged when accessing your home equity by way of a refinance or line of credit, so make sure to include those expenses in your calculations. Are your assets being used for the highest and best purpose? This should be a question you ask yourself frequently.

Another strategy would be to take the $200,000 from a direct recognition asset, such as mutual funds, stocks, money market accounts, or CDs, and use it as down payments for three properties valued at $200,000 each—or one valued at $600,000. Assuming both options would have earned 6% per year, you now have $600,000 earning 6% rather than $200,000. Yes, it's true you will have a mortgage, but those expenses would come out of the additional $24,000 per year of earnings. You gave up the earning power of $200,000 worth of assets in exchange for the earning power of $600,000 worth of assets. For the right person, strategies such as this can be a great way to grow wealth.

REAL ESTATE PROFITS WITHOUT THE WORK

Big benefits come with real estate investing, but it can also come with big headaches. If you're buying rental properties, there's always the possibility of bad markets, bad cash flows, and bad tenants. So, like all good investing, it's best to diversify into different types of properties in different locations. It adds to the safety, but it also adds to the expense. Is there an easy, efficient way to invest without the expense—and risk?

Yes, and it's quite easy. You can gain all the benefits of real estate by investing in exchange-traded funds (ETFs) and real estate investment trusts (REITs). Both allow easy access to real estate. What's the difference, and how do you benefit?

ETFs are similar to mutual funds because they're single companies that own shares of many others. However, unlike mutual funds, ETFs trade like shares of stock on an exchange. With the same ease of buying shares of Apple or Google, you can buy an ETF. However, each ETF owns a basket of stocks, so by purchasing one ETF, you're instantly controlling shares of many different companies. For instance, the Real Estate Select Sector Fund (XLRE) tracks the performance of publicly traded real estate companies in the S&P 500 index, which are among the largest and best managed in the world. By making a single purchase with the ticker symbol XLRE, you'll instantly control shares of companies that develop and manage every aspect of real estate, including homes, rental units, and shopping malls. There are hundreds of real estate ETFs, and you can even find ones specializing in foreign markets, hotels, entertainment, and theme parks. If you can imagine it, it's probably available. If you want exposure to real estate, you don't need to actually buy properties, but you do need to know where to look—and understand what you're buying. ETFs, however, get even more creative. Sometimes the ETF isn't designed to benefit from rising prices, but instead, falling prices.

REAL ESTATE INVESTMENT TRUSTS (REITS)

Real estate has been a key reason for much of wealth created throughout the world, and that's why it should be a big part of any portfolio. The factory only made so much land, but as populations rise, needs grow, and demands increase, more and more people are demanding property. Real estate, of course, is expensive, and few people can afford a diversified basket of properties, especially if you want to include shopping malls, office complexes, and theme parks. Even if you could afford such a portfolio, you'd spend your days researching, negotiating, renovating, leasing, and managing properties—not to mention repairing roller coasters. It's a problem, but if it's a true need, someone will figure out a solution. After all, necessity is the mother of invention—even when it comes to solving real estate investing problems.

In 1960, President Eisenhower allowed for a new approach to income-producing real estate through the creation of the real estate investment trust, or REIT, pronounced as "reet." For the first time, investors could capitalize on income-producing properties that they normally wouldn't have been able to afford or maintain.

PUBLIC VERSUS PRIVATE: WHICH REIT IS BEST?

REITs come in two basic forms—public and private. Public REITs are the ones most investors are familiar with, as they trade on a national exchange, like the New York Stock Exchange (NYSE) or Nasdaq. However, there are also private REITs, which are conceptually the same idea, but they don't trade on an exchange. For the most part, you'll only want to stick with public REITs, but it's important to understand the differences.

You can think of a private REIT as businesses that raise money privately, so investors can pool their money for bigger purchases. However—and this is the kicker—private REITs can usually only be sold to institutional investors, such as banks, pension funds, or hedge funds. However, individuals can also buy them but may need to qualify as an *accredited investor*, which the government deems to be true if you have a net worth of at least one million dollars, excluding your primary residence. You must also have income greater than $200,000 for the past two years ($300,000 if married). The idea is that if you have this kind of wealth, you're probably pretty astute at investing. It's not necessarily a good assumption, and it's why many investors get into trouble by investing in things they don't understand. But even if you qualify and wish to venture into a private REIT, there are things you must know.

First, private REITs are sold by broker-dealers who will charge high commissions. Second, because they're not exchange traded, there's a lack of transparency, which means investors are never quite sure how their money is being used. Many news reports have surfaced showing instances where private REITs mismanaged money by using it for personal gains such as investing in their cousin's rental properties in exchange for kickbacks. Third, and most important, private REITs usually underperform public REITs by about 3.5 percentage points, so you must ask why you should pay high commissions for something that's not transparent and will probably underperform a public REIT. So, with few exceptions, it's best to avoid private REITs, but they're important to understand in case someone tries to sell you one. If it's not exchange traded, it's private.

PUBLIC REITS

Public REITs trade on a public exchange, such as the NYSE or Nasdaq, and you can buy and sell them just as easily as shares of stock. Consequently, you'll sometimes hear them called "real estate stocks." Many of the Real Estate ETFs are funds investing in REITs. Regardless of the structure, investing in public REITs allows you to get real estate exposure without the associated risks, such as heavy debt, rent collections, or property management. The REIT does it all for you. Think of REITs as the "mutual funds" of the real estate market. By purchasing a single REIT, you're controlling the shares of many real estate companies.

Just as there are many types of real estate investments, there are many types of REITs. First, there is the "equity REIT," sometimes called EREIT, which specializes in buying, renting, and selling properties. These could be homes or apartments, but they could also be shopping malls or office complexes. Another type is a "mortgage REIT" or MREIT, which specializes in mortgages and interest on loans. Most REITs use combinations of the two, and you'll sometimes hear them called "hybrid REITs." REITs get special tax breaks and do not pay corporate income tax. Instead, the profits are distributed to investors on a pretax basis. Consequently, REITs usually have higher yields than stocks, but remember, that doesn't mean they're better. They just have more risk, so there's the potential for more return. REITs must pass many tests to qualify, including the following:

- Must be structured as a corporation with fully transferable shares

- Must have at least one hundred shareholders and must have fewer than 50% of the outstanding shares concentrated in the hands of five or fewer shareholders during last half of each taxable year

- Must distribute at least 90% of its annual taxable income, excluding capital gains, as dividends to its shareholders

- Must have at least 75% of its assets invested in real estate, mortgage loans, and shares in other REITs, cash, or government securities

- Must derive at least 75% of its gross income from rents, mortgage interest, or gains from the sale of real property. At least 95% must come from these sources, together with dividends, interest, and gains from securities sales

- Cannot have more than 20% of its assets consist of stocks in taxable REIT subsidiaries

- Less than 30% of gross income can come from sale of real property held for less than four years

REIT funds can focus on different aspects of the real estate market. For instance, VNQ invests in other REITs but also on commercial properties such as shopping malls, office buildings, hotels, and other large projects. If you're looking for international exposure, the company has a related fund called Vanguard Global ex-US Real Estate ETF (VNQI), which is the same idea as VNQ, but it's only for properties outside of the United States. Using funds like this is a beautiful way to gain immediate international real estate diversification without the headaches of having to actually buy properties around the world.

The Dow Jones US Real Estate Index (IYR) focuses on large-cap real estate companies. The term "large-cap" is short for *large capitalization*, which is the overall value, or market capitalization, of the company. It's found by taking the current share price and multiplying by the number of shares outstanding. Large-cap stocks have a total value greater than five billion dollars.

iShares Cohen and Steers REIT ETF (ICF) invests in large real estate companies that are the key players in their respective sectors. It tracks an index made up of US REITs. For instance, for shopping malls, it may invest in Simon Property Group (SPG), but for storage facilities it may choose Public Storage REIT (PSA). Regardless of what's in the fund, you can be sure they're among the most prominent players in the real estate markets.

The SPDR Dow Jones REIT ETF (RWR) tracks the performance of the Dow Jones US Select REIT Index, which is designed to provide a measure of real estate securities that serve as proxies for direct real estate investing. The fund invests at least 80% of its assets in the securities making up the index. These are just a small sample of the many different REITs available, but no matter which you choose, they do the work, and you'll share in the profits.

TRACKING ERRORS: WHY DON'T THINGS ADD UP?

If you invest in a REIT, you may find that the performance doesn't quite match that of the index, which is called the *tracking error*. For example, you may find that an index is up 10% at the end of the year, but the REIT that tracks it is up only 9.95%. Several reasons can account for this, but the biggest is that the funds charge expenses that are deducted from the performance. Second, the REIT may not exactly mirror the stocks in an index. Some stocks may represent a super small percentage of the index, so it may not be worthwhile for the fund to include it in the REIT. Because of this, you'll usually find small discrepancies between the indexes and the REITs. That's not due to an accounting miscalculation or because the secretary was skimming profits. It's because of tracking errors. If you're researching online, all REITs will report tracking errors. It's a good idea to see what they've been historically, so you'll have a better understanding of what to expect.

WATCH FOR RISING INTEREST RATES

Whether you're using ETFs (exchange-traded funds) or ETNs (exchange-traded notes), you must keep an eye on interest rates. They're not the most thrilling things to watch, but you must at least keep up with the trends. Why?

When interest rates rise, most financial asset prices will fall. Bond prices will fall, and in most cases, stock prices will too. That's because higher interest rates mean it's more expensive for companies to borrow to grow their business, so that'll tend to decrease profits. If profits are expected to fall, stock prices follow. Real estate is no exception. It's particularly sensitive to rising interest rates, just as anyone who's ever had an adjustable-rate mortgage can testify. A one-percentage-point increase in rates can mean a significant increase in monthly payments and total interest paid. Again, it's usually because of the leverage. If there's a large mortgage, small increases in interest rates mean large increases in expenses.

REIT prices work the same way for the same reasons. Rising interest rates will sharply cut into profits, and REIT prices can sink. If profits are shrinking, dividend payouts are also reduced, so if you're buying REITs for monthly income, be sure you're not in the midst of a rising interest rate cycle. It's not hard to do, as you can scan financial websites from analysts or comments from the Federal Reserve about the future direction of interest rates. If they're expected to head higher, it may be best to put REIT purchases on hold.

Real estate is an essential part of any investor's portfolio. It's hard to name many multimillionaires—or billionaires—who didn't earn a large part of their wealth from real estate. Historically, it has provided some of the greatest returns for investors, but it also serves as a great hedge when other investments—such as stocks and bonds—may be falling. The important thing to know is that you don't have to buy property in order to profit. The financial markets provide hundreds of REITs, ETFs, and ETNs for you to get fast, efficient ways to gain exposure without the costs or hassles. In a matter of seconds, you can gain domestic or international real estate exposure, whether in homes, rentals, office complexes, shopping malls, and lending companies. It's all there in the financial markets, provided you know where to look.

Strategy in Action

Here is an example that may help you visualize a path to own real estate as an investment.

Mike and Amanda were in their midforties and had always talked about owning real estate as an investment. They worked hard, paid down most of their debt, and saved monthly into their retirement accounts. While they were comfortable financially, they couldn't shake the desire to incorporate real estate into their financial strategy.

They had aggressively paid down their mortgage, and the property had appreciated a lot in recent years. As a result, they had a $400,000 loan on a million-dollar property. They had realized that the $600,000 equity in their home was not working for them as efficiently as it could. They were confused because they had thought for years a top priority should always be to pay off your house as quickly as possible. While paying down your house is a great goal, the equity was not working for them. Their million-dollar home would appreciate at the same rate regardless of if they have a mortgage. They decided to unlock some of their home equity in order to accomplish other financial goals. Assuming they could get up to 80% of their home value as an equity line, that would free up $400,000 for them to invest. Eighty percent of their current home value was $800,000, and if you subtract the current mortgage balance, they were left with $400,000 in equity.

Mike and Amanda worked with their bank and were approved for a $400,000 equity line. Leaning to the conservative side, they only used $300,000 to make real estate investments. This would leave an extra $100,000 available on their equity line for any unexpected events or emergencies. After researching the local real estate market, Mike and Amanda found homes in the $300,000 price range they could rent for $1,600 per month. They used the $300,000 from their equity line to put a $100,000 down payment on three properties. They immediately had over 30% equity in each property and found renters after a couple of months. After paying the mortgage and other expenses, they made around $400 per month from each property. They can use the extra $1,200 per month to pay down the equity line that they used to buy the properties.

In addition, they now have $900,000 worth of real estate, and it cost them only $300,000. They will receive depreciation on those properties that will help lower their tax bill, and even though they paid only $300,000, they will receive appreciation on the full $900,000 worth of real estate. If this type of strategy is executed wisely, it is hard to argue with it.

Quick disclaimer: If you start down this road, it is important that you make wise investment decisions with the equity you unlock. If you take the equity and blow it on a risky stock pick, you will still owe $800,000 on your house but will have lost your equity. You also risk the ability to refinance in the future if your home value falls below a certain point. Also, make sure to include expenses incurred to refinance your home when crunching the numbers.

Chapter 8 Summary

1. **Real estate investing can be rewarding if executed correctly.** Do not underestimate the value of learning from others before jumping in.

2. **Understand the term non-direct-recognition asset.** Some assets will give you the same rate of return whether you own it free and clear or have debt on the asset. Imagine owning one house worth $500k that produces 10% return per year or owning two houses worth $500k that you owe $250k on that each produce 10% per year. Great equity in both situations, but you own $1M worth of assets in the second scenario and only $500k in the first.

3. **Real estate can be a triple-threat investment:**
   a. You have upside potential if the investment grows in value.
   b. You can receive a tax benefit for owning the real estate.
   c. The property has the ability to generate income while you own it.

4. **Understand the 1031 exchange.** Current tax law allows you to roll gains from one property into another and continue to kick the tax can down the road. There are hoops to jump through, but this is a heavily utilized tax strategy.

5. **There are many ways to invest in real estate:**
   a. You can buy real estate directly and own the property.
   b. You can buy real estate with a group of people and realize some of the return with potentially less work and risk.
   c. You can purchase a real estate mutual fund or index that requires little to no effort from you.

Real estate investors still need financial plans and an advisor that is not going to try to talk them out of real estate at every turn. Investing in the stock market is not the only way to secure your financial future. Many of our clients own real estate but still need help creating tax strategies, estate plans, and protecting their assets. Don't ignore creative advice for fear of being pushed to buy something. Connect with my team.

InvestLegacy.com

CHAPTER 9

Traditional IRA versus Roth IRA

T he math isn't hard to figure out. If you want to secure a better retirement, you must put money aside, and the sooner the better. What *is* hard to figure out is how to go about it. Lots of ways exist to put money aside, and lots of nitty-gritty details can make one choice better than another. Regardless of the types of investments or strategies, you need an account to hold your investments. For most investors, an individual retirement account (IRA) is a great solution.

However, within the family of IRA accounts, there are several types, such as the traditional IRA, Roth IRA, and the self-directed IRA. Other versions, such as the SEP IRA (simplified employee pension) and SIMPLE IRA (Savings Incentive Match Plan for Employees), were created for employers to start IRA accounts for employees in exchange for tax benefits from the government.

For most people, the two most commonly known are the traditional IRA and the Roth IRA. When it comes to retirement investing, too many financial planners automatically suggest the Roth IRA because you'll get to withdraw your money tax-free at retirement. It sounds like the perfect plan—who doesn't like tax-free money? But like all financial decisions, the success depends on many factors. For IRAs, one of the biggest risks is for investors to not have *tax diversification*. You already know that you don't want to have all your eggs in one basket, and good retirement planning shows you don't want all of your dollars sitting in one type of account. Still, do-it-yourself investors do it all the time. No one wants to pay tax now, so they fund accounts that will give them a tax deduction today and kick the can down the road. Unfortunately, if tax rates trend up over time, it may be in your best interest to pay the tax now and let your investment grow over time tax-free. Unless you want to take the risk of guessing what your income, tax bracket—and tax laws—will be upon retirement, it's best to aim for three retirement buckets: tax-free, tax-deferred, and taxable (long-term capital gains treatment). What looks like a good decision today can quickly be diminished by one small change in the tax laws tomorrow.

If there's one mistake I see most often with new clients, this is it. They've socked away a lot of money, but it would have been much more advantageous to have it in a different type of account—or diversified across all three.

If there's one mistake I see most often with new clients, this is it. They've socked away a lot of money, but it would have been much more advantageous to have it in a different type of account—or diversified across all three. So let's take a look at the main choices you'll have for setting up retirement accounts, along with information to help you make better choices. Remember, when it comes to investing, time is your biggest asset, and your money's going to be sitting there a long time. It needs to be in the right type of account if your strategy's going to work the right way. Make the right decision today, because after twenty or more years of investing, you'll find the penalties are big for wishing you had known about this sooner.

IRA: TO DEFER OR NOT DEFER?

The individual retirement account, or IRA, is a type of brokerage account which was established under the Employee Retirement Income Security Act (ERISA) in response to concerns for employees without pension plans. The idea was to encourage low-income earners to save, but IRAs quickly became a target for the wealthy to defer taxes. Interestingly, the law used to not allow employees with pensions to open IRAs, but the Carter administration opened them to everyone in 1981.

Congress, in response, created the Tax Reform Act of 1986, which said that only those without pensions or those earning less than $35,000 ($50,000 for married couples) could have savings tax deferred. The earliest you can withdraw from an IRA without paying the 10% penalty is age 59½, but minimum distributions must occur by age 72. After all, the money was never taxed, and Uncle Sam is only going to wait so long for his share. Not surprisingly, strong debates arose surrounding the fairness of employees whose income was outside of these earnings ranges, as well as the required minimum distribution age. Most inventions arise from necessity, and that's how the Roth IRA was created. It solved many of the problems surrounding traditional IRAs.

ROTH IRA: THE DIFFERENCE IS HOW THEY'RE TAXED

The Roth IRA can be created, funded, and invested in just like a traditional IRA. From that perspective, there's no difference between the two types other than the account name.

The Roth IRA was introduced by William Roth (R-Del.) under the Taxpayer Relief Act of 1997. With a Roth IRA, you invest *after-tax* dollars and never pay capital gains or taxes on any of the investments. Also, because the money has already been taxed, there's no minimum mandatory distribution at age seventy-two. If you've held the investments for at least five years, you can withdraw your contributions without penalty. The Roth IRA allows your investments to grow tax-free, and you can withdraw dollar for dollar to meet your expenses without having to worry about taxes. Think about that for a moment—no taxes at all upon withdrawal.

Should you be lucky enough to pick great investments, you could theoretically turn relatively small contributions into a multimillion-dollar account and not owe one cent in taxes. With a Roth IRA, your contributions are not tax deductible though, and that can make a difference for those in higher tax brackets. This is the decision breaker, and unfortunately, most financial planners don't consider it. It turns out, young workers with higher incomes may be better off using traditional IRAs and taking the tax deductions today but pushing taxes far into the future when they're presumably in a lower tax bracket. This also allows their contributions to enjoy tax-deferred compounding over time:

IRA Type	Tax Deferred	Tax Deductible	Tax-Free Withdrawals
TRADITIONAL	YES	YES	NO
ROTH	NO	NO	YES

However, if you're nearing retirement, you're not going to gain a big advantage by deferring the taxes because your tax bracket probably won't change significantly. To contribute to any IRA—traditional or Roth—you must have earned income. In other words, you can't be unemployed and make IRA contributions. Typically, unearned income from pensions or Social Security doesn't count. However, for married couples, if one has earned income but the spouse doesn't, IRA contributions can be made on behalf of the nonworking spouse.

For 2020, the maximum you can contribute to any IRA is the lesser of $6,000 or your earned income for the year. However, for those ages fifty and older, the law allows a $1,000 "catch-up" provision to help those who may have fallen behind in retirement planning. If you're fifty or older, you may contribute the lesser of $7,000 or your earned income for the year.

While there are several types of IRAs, I want to cover only the main ones used by individuals: traditional IRA, Roth IRA, and the self-directed IRA. Virtually anyone can open one up, free of charge, with the same ease as opening a brokerage or checking account. Nearly any financial institution can open an IRA, so you'll find firms like TD Ameritrade, E*Trade, Charles Schwab, Fidelity, and most banks that can quickly create the account. However, the bigger brokers generally offer nearly an unlimited number of choices of assets you can put into the account. Banks, however, usually limit you to certificates of deposit (CDs), which have very low historical returns. Inflation is going to eat away any gains you have, which is why most investing professionals call CDs, half-jokingly, certificates of depreciation.

You're not limited to just one type of IRA, so you could have one of each if you desired, and there are good reasons for doing so, which I'll cover shortly. However, understand that for any given type, you're not required to open a new account each year.

For instance, if you open a Roth IRA for 2019, you don't need to open a new Roth IRA for 2020. Instead, each year's contributions can be made into one account, and it's generally best to do so. That way, you'll have more money to invest, which opens the doors to investing in more expensive assets as well as better diversification. Think how limiting it would be to have ten different Roth IRA accounts, each with $5,000, as opposed to one Roth IRA with $50,000. Yet people make this mistake all the time. When they hear it's time to make the IRA contributions for the year, they assume they must open a new account. However, if you do have multiple accounts of the same type, you can roll them into one, but for now, just realize that you don't need to open a separate account each year. Instead, just be sure to make the contributions.

Once the account is opened, you can choose from many types of investments ranging from stocks, bonds, mutual funds, exchange-traded funds (ETFs), exchange-traded notes (ETNs), and options. The possibilities are nearly endless. You can even deposit cash and let it sit there like a savings account until you're ready to make a purchase.

SELF-DIRECTED IRAS

You may have heard you can buy real estate, precious metals, or other exotic investments in an IRA. Technically, it's true, but that requires what's called a self-directed IRA (SDIRA), which is different from the traditional and Roth IRAs mentioned above, even though they're both self-directed. I know it's confusing. Just realize that if you want a self-directed IRA, it must say that on the account title. Making all the investment decisions by yourself isn't what makes it qualified.

If you open a self-directed IRA, you can own actual real estate, gold bars and bullion, commodities, private placements, tax lien certificates, franchise businesses, and other alternative investments, such as Bitcoin. Within these self-directed IRAs, you can also create them as a traditional or Roth IRA.

Interesting as they may sound, you can't just open a self-directed IRA through a broker, bank, or credit union. Instead, you must go through a custodian or trustee that specializes in these accounts.

With proper financial planning, there can be huge advantages, tax breaks, and diversification.

Here are a couple examples of how I have seen clients utilize self-directed IRAs.

- One of my clients was uneasy about the stock market as he neared retirement and wanted to diversify his portfolio with other assets. He was good friends with a successful home builder, so he negotiated a deal to loan money from his self-directed IRA to the builder. The builder did not have to jump through the hoops with the bank to get money, and my client received 10% per year from the builder. In addition, my client was in first position on the property, so if the builder could not pay, he would have recovered his money from the property.

- Another client I worked with was a very successful real estate investor. She did not like to talk about Roth or traditional IRAs. In her mind, those accounts had to own stock, bonds, or mutual funds, and she knew how to make more money with real estate. I told her that these accounts were not limited to those types of investments and that she was missing out on tax benefits. After working through various scenarios, she started funding IRAs for the first time and is now using those accounts to buy additional real estate. The main difference is the real estate she buys with her Roth IRA will enjoy tax-free growth and withdrawals.

As you can see from these examples, the clients still loaned money and bought real estate. They just did so in a much more tax-efficient way. It is amazing how a few adjustments to their strategy made a significant difference.

There are potential pitfalls to self-directed IRAs if you don't know what you are doing. For instance, if you finance a property to put into a self-directed IRA, you can create what's called *unrelated business taxable income*. Further, you can't put your own labor or "sweat equity" into the property, and all expenses must be paid from the IRA's funds. If you mow the lawn of your rental property that's inside your IRA, it could count as a distribution and trigger tax consequences—and penalties on the entire account. Self-dealing transactions, which are those that bring personal gain to the account holder prior to retirement, are also prohibited. If you buy rare coins from yourself to put into the IRA, that would be a self-dealing transaction. Living in a rental property that's held in the account would also disqualify it. The list is long, and the consequences are potentially steep. Like all strategies, if implemented correctly, self-directed IRAs can tip the odds in your favor.

DANGER: WHAT NOT TO BUY IN A ROTH IRA

While exposure to just about any asset can be put into an IRA, it doesn't mean they're all good choices. Probably the biggest mistake for do-it-yourselfers is to buy municipal bonds, also called muni-bonds, or "munis," in a Roth IRA. These bonds are usually issued by local governments to finance public roads, schools, airports, and other facilities needed by the public. As a result, these bonds are tax exempt, which may sound like it's great for an investment. However, because they're tax exempt, their yields are lower than comparable taxable bonds. Because interest and capital gains are already exempt in an IRA, there's no benefit from buying munis. You're only hurting yourself by accepting lower yields without the tax benefits. However, other bonds may be well suited for IRAs, especially as you near retirement and want to go into protection mode. For example, let's say you buy a bond fund outside of an IRA. The fund has a 4% yield, but it'll be reduced to 3% if you're in the 25% tax bracket. If you hold that fund in an IRA, however, you'll avoid those taxes, and that means your real rate of return will be higher.

THE BACKDOOR ROTH

Based on the previous discussions, it's not hard to see that a Roth IRA can provide great incentives for retirement savings. However, not everyone can open a Roth IRA because there are income limits for the Roth—but not the traditional IRA. For 2020, you can make full contributions to a Roth IRA if your modified adjusted gross income (MAGI) is less than $124,000. If you're married and file jointly, your MAGI must be under $206,000.

However, if your income is greater than these levels, you're allowed to make *partial contributions*, which gradually decrease as the income level rises, until it's phased out completely. The IRS provides a table of income levels and contribution limits for singles and married couples that usually changes somewhat each year. For instance, in 2020, if you're a single filer with income greater than $124,000 but less than $125,500, you can contribute $5,400 rather than the $6,000 maximum. If you qualify for the catch-up contribution, you could contribute $6,300 rather than $7,000. At the upper limit, if you earn $137,500, you can contribute $600, or $700 if you qualify for the catch-up contribution. Above $139,000, you can't contribute a single dollar. There's a similar tiered structure for married couples. The limits aren't important for now, other than to show that after certain income levels, you can't contribute to a Roth IRA—at least in the traditional way. There is, however, a way through the back door.

HOW TO CREATE A BACKDOOR ROTH IRA

A backdoor Roth isn't a special type of account, so don't walk into your broker's office saying, "Hey, I'd like to open a backdoor Roth!" Instead, it's a roundabout way of opening a Roth IRA that sidesteps the income requirements. It's perfectly legal, and any broker can assist with the process.

The basic idea is to open a traditional IRA, which anyone can do because there are no income limits. However, since 2010, the IRS imposes no income limits on who can *convert* a traditional IRA to a Roth. A conversion just means there's some paperwork you fill out to change the status of the account, much like you could change a single checking account to a joint checking. Just fill out the forms and voilà—you've got a Roth IRA. So, once you fund the traditional IRA, simply convert it into a Roth IRA.

Alternatively, you can roll the traditional IRA into an existing Roth IRA. For instance, perhaps you had a Roth long before your income levels precluded you from contributing. In that case, just shift the assets of your newly opened traditional IRA to your existing Roth. If you open a Roth by converting a traditional IRA, you will owe taxes. Remember, the money put into a traditional IRA is pretax. If you roll it into a Roth, you'll owe taxes on that money. For example, if you make the full $6,000 contribution to the traditional IRA and then convert it to a Roth, you'll owe taxes on $6,000. The backdoor Roth doesn't escape the tax, but at the same time, it doesn't create any tax penalties. It's the same tax you would have paid had you been allowed to open the Roth IRA in the first place. The backdoor Roth just sidesteps the income requirements.

WHICH IS BETTER?

Now that you have a basic understanding of the differences between the traditional and Roth IRA, you probably have a burning question—which is better? It's an easy question but a difficult answer. Like all financial decisions, it depends on assumptions. If one were truly better than the other across all assumptions, there'd be no reason to have the two types. Instead, you want to ask, "Which is better for me?" So let's break down the two types and look at the benefits and drawbacks. The first hurdle to cross is whether you're eligible or not. If your income is too high for a Roth, and you don't want to go through the trouble of a backdoor Roth, you have no choice but to fund a traditional IRA. Assuming, however, that you do have a choice, the primary consideration is whether you'll be better off taking tax breaks today or at retirement.

The traditional IRA's biggest benefit is that you get to fund it with pretax dollars. That means your contributions aren't taxed—at least not yet. Therefore, more of your money goes to work, and

The traditional IRA's biggest benefit is that you get to fund it with pretax dollars.

that maximizes the compounding effect. The easiest way to understand this is to assume you receive a $5,000 bonus from your employer. If you're using a traditional IRA, you can contribute the entire amount. On the other hand, if you want to use a Roth, you must pay taxes first. If you're in the 25% bracket, $1,250 comes off the top, which leaves $3,750 for your contribution—much less than $5,000. We can look at it another way. Perhaps you'd make a $5,000 contribution in the Roth anyway. Well, that means you'd need to earn $6,667 so that you'll have $5,000 after taxes. No matter how you cut it, contributing with after-tax dollars is a drawback. The traditional IRA advantage goes even further. Because your current income is reduced, you'll owe less tax today. So, while everyone likes to tout the "no taxes at retirement" benefit for the Roth, you can see there are potentially some serious benefits with a traditional IRA.

If you're a high-income earner and have a long time until retirement, you may be better off with a traditional IRA. You'll be taxed on the money when you withdraw it at retirement, but presumably, you'll be in a lower tax bracket. However, that's the big risk. There's no guarantee you'll be in a lower tax bracket, especially if you're decades away from retirement. There's a related risk with receiving your tax benefits today with a traditional IRA; it's easier to spend the money on things other than retirement. To balance out the benefits with the Roth, you'd have to invest your annual tax savings back into a retirement plan, and it's unlikely for that to happen every year for decades.

For the Roth, you'll owe taxes on the money before you make your contributions. That's the big downside. However, the good news is that no matter how much money you earn from your investments, you'll never owe taxes when you withdraw the money at retirement. Don't let that be the sole determinant. There are plenty of scenarios that can be painted where you'd come out ahead with a traditional IRA. Another Roth advantage is that it may force you to save more money because it gives you less money in your pocket today. Remember, with the traditional IRA, you're not paying taxes on the contributions today, so that provides more money in your pocket. Rather than using that extra money to further save for retirement, people tend to spend it. If you're not a great saver, the Roth may give you a mathematical advantage by forcing you to save it.

ADDITIONAL ROTH BENEFITS

Despite the pros and cons of each type of account, there are some other factors that make a Roth particularly attractive. First, the Roth is more flexible if you must withdraw money early. While it's never advisable to tap into your retirement savings, no one can predict the future, and you might find yourself in a position to consider withdrawal. Any of your *contributions* can be withdrawn at any time with no taxes or penalties. However, if you're withdrawing any *earnings*, you can only do so under certain qualifications.

First, you must have had the Roth for at least five years, and the time begins at the beginning of the first year's contribution. Next, you must be at least 59½ years old, disabled, or using up to $10,000 toward the purchase of a first home. Death also qualifies, in which case the distribution can be made by your heirs. For example, let's say you contributed $6,500 for 2018 and 2019, for a total of $13,000. In 2020, the account has grown to $15,000. You could withdraw up to $13,000 without taxes or penalties, but if you withdrew any amount over that, they'd have to qualify based on the above conditions.

Roth IRAs don't have required minimum distributions at age seventy-two. In fact, they're the only tax-advantaged accounts that don't. So, if you want to pass money onto heirs or charities, a Roth can be a perfect solution.

RETIREMENT STRATEGY: TRADITIONAL AND ROTH

Up to this point, I've shown that the key factor for choosing one type of IRA over the other is the timing of the taxes. Whether you're using a traditional or Roth, you're going to pay taxes. It's just a matter of when. By choosing one over the other, you're making assumptions about future tax rates, and that's a big assumption. Like all good financial strategies, when in doubt, split them up. If you don't see a clear benefit, consider using both. You can have as many IRA accounts as you'd like, but you must stay within the contribution limits.

You could, for example, contribute $6,500 to a single traditional IRA, but you could also contribute $3,500 to a traditional and $3,000 to a Roth. When you use a Roth, you're effectively locking in today's tax rates in exchange for knowing you won't be taxed at higher rates in the future. But what if the rates are lower? Now your plan backfired. By using both types of accounts, you're getting a partial tax break today and a partial one at retirement. It's a tax-diversification strategy that's likely to prove superior for most people.

If tax rates are lower than expected, you can take your withdrawals from the traditional IRA and let the Roth continue to grow tax-free. On the other hand, if rates are higher, even if just for a few years, you can either make withdrawals from the Roth, or you could take a little from each. That way, you can access the amount of money you need each year but greatly reduce the tax burden. Like all diversification strategies, you're giving up the potential for having great benefits in exchange for not ending up with the wrong one. You'll have a high-probability plan that's acceptable. Diversification works for growing your investments toward retirement, but it also works for getting the cash back to you at retirement.

If there were a way to know the future tax rates, the decision would be a lot easier, but we don't, so diversifying your future withdrawals into different tax buckets is the next best thing. For some people, using a traditional and Roth IRA can be a great solution. Remember, if your income doesn't allow you to open a Roth, use a traditional IRA, and then convert to a backdoor Roth.

2020 Strategy

In my line of work, I get asked every day, "What would you do if you were in my shoes?" Everyone's situation is different, and therefore, their plan should be specific to them. But let's talk through how this chapter could be applied into today's market and tax environment.

The current administration has created a historically low tax environment, but our national debt has continued to rise. Many of my clients worry that tax rates have to increase dramatically in the future to pay down the debt while keeping up with entitlements that the government has promised to people. In addition, Social Security is not keeping up with the rate of withdrawal, and on its current path, benefits may be reduced in the not-too-distant future. New tax reform floating around would increase tax rates, capital gains rates, corporate tax rates, and more. So how do we protect our retirement and other investments when there is so much uncertainty? I believe that tax rates will trend up in the future, but depending on when someone wants to retire, we can't predict if they will be near the top or heading back down when they need money.

So in today's environment, we are recommending that clients aggressively build their Roth IRA and taxable investment account to catch up with the traditional IRA funds they have been building for years. Our goal is for our clients to have a meaningful amount of money in all three tax buckets: tax-deferred, tax-free, and taxable. If they can accomplish this, it will allow us to control their tax rate in retirement. Here's how we can do that.

If we have all three buckets, we can decide where to pull money, depending on tax rates, when they need it. For example, if a client retires halfway through a year and has a good amount of income, we may decide to use their Roth IRA for the rest of the year to keep their tax rate down. In their first full year of retirement, we could then begin taking funds from the traditional IRA but only to the level that we want to pay tax. At that point, the Roth and taxable investment account would jump back in.

Let me drive home this point again. The type of investments you buy is very important. However, it is not all you should think about. Knowing what type of account to fund and buy the investments within is equally important. Tax diversification should not be overlooked.

Many of my new clients seek out my team as a result of our proactive tax strategies. In the next chapter, I will share concepts you need to know about today!

Chapter 9 Summary

1. **Tax-free is not always better than tax-deferred, and tax-deferred is not always better than tax-free.** Use the details specific to your situation to determine if you use one or the other, or a combination of both.

2. **Self-directed IRAs are a powerful option that is often misunderstood.** The idea that you can purchase real estate, give loans, or even directly invest in start-up companies surprises most people. You need to make sure it is executed correctly to avoid unnecessary fees or penalties.

3. **Backdoor Roth and Roth 401(k)s:** There are ways to invest in tax-free accounts even if you think your income disqualifies you. Both of these strategies can help you shelter funds tax-free even if you have high income.

CHAPTER 10

Tax Strategies: Stop Overpaying

I can say with a high level of confidence that you are paying too much in taxes. As Federal Appeals Court Judge Billings Learned Hand famously said in 1934, "Anyone may arrange his affairs so that his taxes shall be as low as possible. Nobody owes any public duty to pay more than the law demands."

Well said, but the problem is that you don't just choose among ten laws and pick the one that minimizes your taxes. The current tax code is about 2,600 pages long, and the words, acronyms, and legalese make it impossible for most people to find the best path to minimize taxes. Further, each law seems inextricably tied to all others. You may find one law that appears to be the one you're looking for, but it says notwithstanding this, excluding that, or superseding these. You can't just read a tax law and find your answer. Instead, you must see the entire tangled spider web. To make it more challenging, many of these laws will change the following year.

The good news is that the more complex laws get, the harder it is to keep all the links straight, and that's largely what sets up some of the more interesting tax breaks. You must work hard to fight for every penny. Remember, nobody owes any public duty to pay more than the law demands. However, it's not easy to do, but this is where we add a lot of value for clients. In almost every tax return we review, we find many places where a simple adjustment can reduce taxes, and in some cases, sharply reduce them. Tax laws are complex, and people miss the deductions they should be taking. We use our deep network of highly trained CPAs, tax attorneys, and other professionals to implement creative tax strategies for our clients. We stay well within the law while saving our clients as much as possible.

I want to cover various tax-planning terms that will be important for you to know. While you may have heard these terms thrown around in the past, I have found most people do not fully understand how they are impacted by them.

TAX EFFICIENCY

Investments must not only be chosen for their risk levels and potential returns, but you must also consider the impact of taxes, or what's called the *tax efficiency*. Depending on the ETF, ETN, or other type of funds, taxes can be a big expense, possibly bigger than internal fees. It's the after-tax dollars you must watch, because that's the only part you get to keep.

Index funds, for instance, are passively managed, which means there's no skill involved. Investment managers aren't trying to pick the next hot stock, buy at the bottom, or sell at the top. Instead, they just hold a basket of stocks that represents an index. They're trying to replicate the market, not beat it.

When making an investment decision, tax efficiency should

always be on your list of considerations. Unfortunately, most people focus on fees and historical rates of return.

HARVEST TIME: COLLECTING ALL LOSSES

Savvy investors often hold many assets in their portfolios, including ETFs and shares of stock. A great tax strategy is to close any losing positions before the one-year mark but hold your winners for more than a year. Doing so, your gains get long-term tax status, which lowers your tax liability. Depending on the timing, you may also be able to use the short-term losses against those gains. At a minimum, you can certainly use the losses to reduce your taxable income.

Tax harvesting is a strategy used to limit or reduce tax liabilities within a given investment. You look for opportunities to take advantage of market dips to lock in losses for tax-planning purposes. You may love the position but sell it for the short-term loss and then buy it back thirty-one days later. If you buy the same position or one that is substantially identical within thirty days, you may violate the "wash-sale" rule. If you do, the loss can be added to the basis of the position but will not be as beneficial in the short term.

ETFs are great tools for harvesting losses because they can be purchased on specific sectors. This allows you to sell an individual stock but closely replace it with a sector ETF. Doing so, you don't miss out on the exposure but do avoid wash-sale rule violations.

For instance, say you own $10,000 worth of JP Morgan (JPM), and it's worth $9,000 just prior to the one-year anniversary of your purchase. You can sell those shares to get the tax loss but immediately buy the Financial SPDR Sector (XLF), which will still closely track the performance of all financial stocks. In fact, in 2020, JP Morgan represented nearly 11% of the entire ETF. You still get good exposure to financial stocks, but it's far from a perfect substitute, so you won't have to worry about violating the wash-sale rule. The benefit is enormous. For all practical purposes, not much has changed in terms of risk, but you do have a $1,000 loss to apply against your income. How much of a difference does this make?

Let's say the XLF rises 10% after you've held it for one year. Had you just purchased this ETF rather than JP Morgan, you'd have a 10% unrealized gain. However, because you harvested losses, you reduced your taxable income. If you're in the 30% bracket, you reduced income by $300, which is 3% of your $10,000 investment. Your total return is therefore 10% + 3% = 13%. It may not sound like much of a difference, but it's 30% higher. If you're in a relatively high tax bracket and have a portfolio of stocks, the savings can be tens of thousands of dollars. Tax-harvesting strategies are about understanding many small ways to make one big difference.

After the market dropped from COVID-19 in March 2020, we actively harvested losses for our clients but kept them invested in the market. It was a great example of a year that an investor could experience great returns in their accounts while also showing a loss on the tax return. Tax planning doesn't get better than that.

MARGINAL VERSUS AVERAGE TAX RATES

The United States uses a progressive tax system, which means the more you make, the more you pay. However, the money you earn gets taxed at different rates, and there's a lot of confusion on exactly how that works. Below are the marginal tax brackets for 2020. The table only shows ranges for those who are single, but a similar column is usually shown for the married filing jointly. Those ranges will usually be twice that of those filing individually:

2020 TAX BRACKET	TAXABLE INCOME (SINGLE)
10%	Up to $9,875
12%	$9,876 to $40,125
22%	$40,126 to $85,525
24%	$85,526 to $163,300
32%	$163,301 to $207,350
35%	$207,351 to $518,400
37%	Over $518,400

Using the above 2020 tax table, if you're single and earned $9,875, you'd owe 10%, or $987.50 in taxes. If, instead, you had earned one extra dollar, that would bump you up the 12% bracket, which makes many people think they'd owe 12% on $9,876, or $1,185.12. If that were true, it would be an expensive dollar to earn since it created an additional $197.62 ($1,185 – $987.50) in taxes.

Fortunately, that's not how the system works. Instead, you're taxed at each rate only for those dollars in that bracket. If you earned one extra dollar beyond $9,875, you'd owe 12% on that *one dollar*. Your tax bill would only increase by twelve cents, which is much more reasonable than $197.62.

A progressive tax system will never leave you with less money because you jumped to a new tax bracket. That would be a terrible tax system because nobody would have the incentive to earn more money. Imagine earning one more dollar but ending up with less money. Unfortunately, many people do believe that's how it works and become cautious about jumping to higher brackets. They end up earning far less money than they could have and wonder why they can't fund their retirement accounts. Don't ever fear higher tax brackets, because paying more taxes only means you made more money. Keep in mind that tax schedules only apply to federal taxes. Most states assess income taxes too, which increases your tax bill further. Only seven states have no income taxes: Alaska, Florida, Nevada, South Dakota, Texas, Washington, and Wyoming. Tennessee and New Hampshire can also be added to this list because they don't tax earned income, but they do currently tax interest and dividends. If you're doing business in a state outside of these seven, you need to take all the tax breaks you can get.

Marginal tax rates are watched closely by economists because they do alter people's incentives to work. Imagine if the highest tax bracket was 99%, and you were in the bracket just below. If a business offers to hire you for a project for which they'll pay $100,000, you'd probably turn it down. The high bracket reduces your incentive to work, but if you did accept the job, it wouldn't leave you with less money. Instead, after paying 99% tax on it, you'd take home only another $1,000.

While marginal rates are important, most decisions are based on the *average tax rate*, which is found by taking your total tax bill and dividing it by your income. For example, let's say you earned $100,000 in 2020. Notice your income falls in the 24% bracket, but remember, that doesn't mean you owe 24% on the entire amount. Instead, you'd owe the full tax on the first three brackets. So, that's 10% on the first $9,875. However, the second bracket only taxes the next $40,125 – $9,875, or $30,250. Therefore, you'd also owe 12% on $30,250, or $3,630. The third bracket taxes the next $45,400 at 22%, so that's another $10,896. So far, you've been taxed on $85,525. Because you earned $100,000, the remaining $14,475 is taxed at 24%, or $4,632. Your total tax bill is therefore $20,145.50. While your marginal tax rate is 24%, your average rate is $20,145.50 ÷ $100,000, or 20.15%. Even though you had some dollars taxed at 10%, 12%, 22%, and 24%, the system is effectively making it as if it were a flat-rate system at 20.15%. Unless you're in the bottom bracket, your average tax rate will always be less than the marginal tax rate. For financial planning, don't worry so much about your marginal tax rate, but instead, how additional earned money will affect your average rate.

ADJUSTED GROSS INCOME

Tax forms always ask for your Adjusted Gross Income (AGI), which is the foundation for determining your taxable income. As the name implies, AGI takes your gross income—the total of all income earned—and subtracts things that are deductible. Common deductions include IRA contributions, health care savings account deductions, alimony, early withdrawal penalties by banks, tuition and student loan interest, and some business expenses.

TAX CREDIT VERSUS TAX DEDUCTION

Generally, a tax deduction lowers your taxable income, but only by the taxes paid. If you're in the 24% tax bracket and have a $1,000 tax deduction, it lowers your taxable income by $240. Tax credits, on the other hand, generally come right off the bottom line. If you have a $1,000 tax credit, it reduces your tax bill by $1,000.

Tax credits fall into one of three categories: refundable, nonrefundable, and partially refundable. Let's say you have a refundable $3,000 tax credit. If it reduces your tax bill to negative $1,000, you'll get $1,000 back. If you had no income for the year, you'd get the entire $3,000 back. On the other hand, if it were nonrefundable, you wouldn't get $1,000 back. You would just get to use $2,000 of the $3,000 tax credit. Finally, if it were partially refundable, you can get a portion of the unused amount back, say $500. For example, the American Opportunity Credit can reduce your tuition costs by up to $2,500. Also, 40% of the credit, or $1,000, is refundable, so you could get that back even if you owe no tax.

STANDARD DEDUCTIONS VERSUS ITEMIZED

The government allows taxpayers to reduce their taxable income by deducting expenses. However, many people don't have a long list of things they can deduct. They work a single job, collect a check, and use that information to file taxes. However, if they really had to think hard, they could probably come up with a list of things that are deductible. The government realizes this and allows people to elect a standard deduction. In 2020, for single taxpayers, the standard deduction is $12,400. For married filing joint, it's $24,800. The government is essentially saying that if everyone had to really think about it, they'd be able to come up with these deductions, so to save the work, they allow you to just choose this standard deduction.

Other people, however, do have a long list of things to deduct—expensive things—and it can pay to go through each one and list them on your tax forms, which is called itemizing expenses. Perhaps you bought a $2,000 computer that's deductible for your business. If you're in the 24% bracket, that would save you $480 in tax. If you itemize, most financial planning software will also calculate your taxes based on the standard deduction, and you're allowed to pick the lowest one.

Itemizing takes a lot of work because you must track all business expenses. If you do run a business, it helps to have a credit card that's dedicated only to business purchases. You'll get a great year-end summary to show to your accountant, which makes itemizing easier. Many phone apps are designed to make it simple by allowing you to snap a photo of a business receipt, which it records, categorizes, and keeps track of the costs. If you have a lot of business expenses, it'll pay to itemize, but that's assuming you keep accurate track of the deductible items.

CAPITAL GAINS: PROFITS FROM BUYING AND SELLING

If you buy low and sell high, that's great. You've got a profit. Unfortunately, you've also got a capital gain on which you'll owe taxes. Capital gains are the profits realized on nearly anything you sell, whether shares of stock, real estate, or a coin collection, for instance. Capital gains come in two forms: unrealized and realized. Let's say you buy shares of stock for $100. That's called your *cost basis*, which is usually just the price paid. However, for some assets, adjustments may be made to this number for tax purposes. Now, let's say the stock price rises to $150. At this point, you've got a $50 *unrealized* gain, which is sometimes called a "paper profit" because it's only on paper. You can't spend that $50 without first selling the shares. However, if you sell them for $150, you'll have a $50 *realized* gain and owe taxes on that amount.

Here's what's subject to capital gains taxes. The IRS defines a capital asset as "almost everything you own and use for personal or investment purposes." That doesn't leave much room for interpretation. The IRS wants a cut of every profit you get. Remember, THE IRS spells *THEIRS*. If you buy a baseball card for $5 and sell it for $10 on eBay, you technically owe taxes on the $5 gain. Capital losses are just the opposite. If you buy a hundred shares at $100 and sell for $90, you have a $10 loss per share, or $1,000 capital loss.

SHORT-TERM AND LONG-TERM CAPITAL GAINS

Capital gains taxes depend on the length of time you've held the investment. If it's one year or less, it's taxed as a short-term capital gain. If it's one year *plus one day*, it's taxed as a long-term capital gain. Be careful of the "plus one day" part. If you sell an asset for a profit on the one-year anniversary, it's still a short-term capital gain.

You're allowed to deduct capital losses against any capital gains, dollar for dollar, provided the losses don't exceed the gains. Typically, short-term gains are matched with short-term losses and long-term gains are matched with long-term losses. If there's still a difference, you net short-term against long-term.

For any short-term gains, you're normally taxed as ordinary income. If you pay $10,000 for shares of stock and sell them for $15,000, it's as if your employer paid you an extra $5,000. Generally speaking, the short-term capital gains taxes are much higher than long term, so a lot of financial planning centers on long-term holdings. It can make an enormous difference in the end.

Capital gains are better than ordinary income for a couple of reasons. First, they're taxed at more favorable rates if held long term. Second, you can control the timing of capital gains, which is something you generally cannot do with income.

For instance, in 2020, long-term capital gains taxes are the lowest they've been since 1933. A single filer earning $40,000 or less pays 0% taxes on long-term capital gains. For incomes between $40,000 and $441,450, you'll pay just 15%. If you're earning more than $441,450, you'll pay a maximum of 20%. Let's say you held the above shares for exactly one year. Your effective tax rate is 24%, you'd owe 24% tax on the $5,000 gain, or $1,200. However, by holding just one more day, you'd be taxed at 15%, or $750. When it comes to capital gains, what a difference a day can make.

Even though there's a great incentive to cash in on highly appreciated assets for long-term gains, especially for the 0% and 15% gains taxes, it's always best to check with a financial advisor.

WITHHOLDINGS: OVER OR UNDER?

Employees are required to fill out a Form W-4 to indicate the amount of taxes that should be withheld from each paycheck. It's tempting to want to overstate the amount so you'll get a nice tax refund at the end of the year. However, from a financial planning standpoint, it's nothing to brag about. First, you're giving the government a free loan. That's money you could have been using or investing during the year. Instead, it's just sitting there, doing nothing, and then you get it back in a year. Second, you're not making the best use of your deductions. Always find the best deductions to put more money in your pocket today—not to get an interest-free return of your money in a year. On the other hand, withholding too little means you could get hit with a larger tax bill than expected. If you can't pay it, you're subject to stiff penalties. Very few financial decisions live at the extremes. The best answer is usually somewhere in the middle. Again, think balance.

STEP RIGHT UP

Some of the best tax strategies rely on holding assets until death. If they're assets you plan to pass to heirs, you're better off leaving the asset upon your death rather than selling and giving them cash while

> **Some of the best tax strategies rely on holding assets until death.**

you're alive. When you hold assets, your heirs receive a *step-up* basis. That means the cost basis of the asset is increased, or stepped up, to the current market value at time of the owner's death. If an heir sells the security for that price, no tax is due.

For instance, let's say your wealthy uncle buys a thousand shares of stock for $20 per share. Upon his death, it's trading for $150 per share, and he leaves them to you. If you sell the shares for $150 per share, or $150,000, you don't owe a single penny in taxes. That's because your cost basis was stepped up to the current $150 market value upon your uncle's death. In the eyes of the law, you bought and sold at $150 per share. On the other hand, if you sell for $160,

WISH I KNEW THAT SOONER

you'd owe taxes on the $10 difference. However, if your uncle had transferred the same shares while he was alive, you'd receive a *carryover basis*, which means his cost basis carries over to you, so your cost basis would be $20 instead of $150.

What if the value of the shares is lower? Just as you can receive a step-up basis, you could also get a *step-down* basis. The important point is that your cost basis is valued at the time of his death. If your uncle's shares were worth $18 at the time of his death, that would be your cost basis instead, and it would be called a step-down basis.

It used to be that people could leave unlimited amounts of tax-free money to heirs. For 2020, the estate and gift tax exemption is $11.58 million per individual, up from $11.4 million in 2019. You can leave $11.58 million to heirs and pay no federal estate or gift tax, while a married couple will be able to shelter $23.16 million. According to the Congressional Research Service economist Jane Gravelle, about half of all capital gains in the United States are never subject to taxation because of the step-up basis law.[11]

ESTATE TAX VERSUS INHERITANCE TAX

Ben Franklin said nothing is certain except death and taxes. But who would have guessed that even after death, taxes live on? The term "death taxes" is a collective term that's used to denote any taxes levied upon one's estate after death. The taxes come in two basic forms: First, an *inheritance tax* is levied on the person who receives the estate or other assets. Second, an *estate tax* is paid by the estate before the assets are transferred. The taxes always get paid; it's just a question of who pays them. Unfortunately, clients often find out the hard way that with just a little bit of estate planning, less money would go to the government, and more would stay with the family. It's an expensive lesson to find out when it's too late to do anything about it.

BUYING THINGS TO REDUCE INCOME

Clients often ask if they should go on spending sprees to reduce taxable income. While there are certainly many tax deductions available for full- or part-time self-employed taxpayers, it never makes sense to spend money unless it's going to put you in a better situation. If you spend just to lower taxable income, you'll end up spending more money than you saved. Sure, you'll have more stuff, but if it wasn't anything you needed, you just put yourself in a worse financial position. If you have an effective tax rate of 20%, and you spend $10 to get a tax deduction, you will save only $2. However, if you would have kept the $10 and paid the tax, you would have been left with $8. Remember, unless it's a tax credit, you only lower income by the marginal tax rate, so you'll always spend more than you save.

However, if there are things you need, and you can make the purchases in time to get tax savings, it can be a good decision. Business owners can take deductions that arise from the normal course of business. To qualify, the goods or services must be primarily for the business and not for personal use. Expenses such as rent, employee wages, retirement plan contributions, inventory, phones, business cards, software, advertising, attorney and account-ing fees, bank fees, professional fees and licenses, vehicle repairs, travel, health insurance, continuing education, bad debts, charitable contributions, and taxes would be common and accepted. The IRS says they must be ordinary and necessary for business, and most important, cannot be extravagant.

If you buy something at the last minute, the postmark is the official date of payment. So if you're mailing a check for a substantial expense, and it's the last business day of the year, be sure it's post-marked for the current year. It's not a bad idea to send it by certified mail, too, so that you have a receipt of the mailing date. As long as the

163

check is mailed in the current year, the goods or services are considered to be paid for that year.

A simple way to reduce taxable income is to maximize retirement savings. For 2020, you can make pretax contributions up to a maximum of $19,500. Those fifty and older can make catch-up contributions of an additional $6,500. Since contributions are made through paycheck deferrals, the money saved in these employer-sponsored retirement accounts is one of the simplest ways to lower your tax bill. Whatever you do, don't spend money unnecessarily just because you're trying to lower your tax bill. There are easier ways where you can benefit greatly.

THE HOME SALE EXCLUSION

Whenever you sell a home, you're generally subjected to capital gains taxes. Under certain conditions, however, unmarried people can exclude up to $250,000 of profits from capital gains while married couples can exclude $500,000. It's done through the home sale exclusion.

Let's say you paid $200,000 for a home and sell it for $440,000. That's a $240,000 capital gain, but it wouldn't have to be reported as taxable income since the $240,000 gain is less than the $250,000 exclusion. However, if you sold it for $460,000, that's a $260,000 capital gain. Because you get to exclude $250,000, you'd just report the additional $10,000 as taxable income. Like most tax laws, there are rules. To qualify for the exclusion, you must pass the two-out-of-five-year rule.

The rule says the property must be your primary residence, not an investment property. You must also have lived there for two of the past five years immediately preceding the sale date. The two years of residence, however, don't have to be consecutive.

You can use this rule to exclude your profits each time you sell your main home, but this means you can claim the exclusion only once every two years because you must spend at least that much time in residence.

RMD STRATEGY

Current tax law requires distributions from most tax-deferred retirement accounts to begin at age seventy-two. This is called a required minimum distribution. The IRS will not let you defer taxes on these funds forever, so they set an age and calculation to force distributions so they can collect taxes. The big question is whether you should wait as long as possible or start your distributions before age seventy-two.

Based on the assumptions used, we have seen many instances where it made sense for clients to begin taking IRA distributions as early as possible even if they didn't need the money. Why would someone take money out of an account and pay taxes if they don't need it? This is where the strategy comes in.

If a client has a low taxable income, and tax rates are historically low, it could be in their best interest to start withdrawing a small amount each year in order to keep those dollars taxed at a very low rate. They can then turn around and reinvest those funds in the market. The alternative would be to wait until age seventy-two and hope tax rates are the same or lower and be forced to take out a larger amount that could push you into a higher tax bracket. Once you hit age seventy-two you have to take out at least what the IRS tells you, so you have much less room for creative strategies.

An entire book could be written on creative tax strategies, and my team really enjoys this arena. Unfortunately, tax law is so fluid that by the time the book is complete, it would have to be updated. The best approach is to have a proactive, creative financial team around you, so you are not missing out. There are few experiences more frustrating than learning you paid more taxes than you needed to, and you found out too late to correct it.

Chapter 10 Summary

1. **If creative tax strategies are not a routine topic of conversation as it pertains to your financial plan, you need to reevaluate your plan.** In my experience, most people are overpaying taxes just because they don't know what they don't know.

2. **Tax-loss harvesting:** Do you believe that you can show a loss on your taxes in the same year you have a great return in your investment account? Proactive tax harvesting is a strategy my team uses to bring additional value to our clients.

3. **Basis step-up:** If you inherit an asset, you will pay tax on the gains above the value on the day you received it. If the asset is gifted to you while the person is living, you will pay tax on gains above the value they originally paid for it. Consider delaying receiving gifts if you don't need the money now.

4. **Two-out-of-five-year rule:** If a home is your primary residence for two out of five years, you are able to sell that home and exclude $250k of gains from taxes if you are single and up to $500k of gains if you are married.

CHAPTER 11

Retirement Planning

A merican entrepreneur Jim Rohn said, "Discipline is the bridge between goals and accomplishment." It's an important reminder that setting goals isn't the real battle. Setting goals is easy. Following through can be a different story. Most retirement plans are generic and oversimplify the process. They're usually cookie-cutter approaches that may work for a lot of people, but they also have potential pitfalls.

My approach allows you to enjoy life today while still making sound retirement decisions. You don't have to plan to retire late into your sixties just because that's what most generic plans suggest. You've seen other people retire in their fifties, and it's not because they're necessarily working harder than you, but they're probably working smarter, making better financial decisions, and most of all, avoiding mistakes. You can do it too.

However, you must be willing to do what it takes. Remember, however, that the sooner your investments begin working, the sooner they create more "employees" for you. The key is to begin today and avoid costly mistakes along the way. No matter how simple or sophisticated a financial strategy may sound, it could fail if emotions become the primary decision maker or you make major mistakes. Rather than getting too concerned with finding "the best" retirement plan, create one that you understand and that you will follow.

SETTING YOUR GPS

Retirement planning is a little bit of science—and a lot of art. The science side includes financial math, lifespan estimates, inflation adjustments, and other assumptions that are easy to determine. But the bigger question is how much money will you really need at retirement?

That's the art side. There's no magic plan that works for everyone, and there's no specific number that's required to get you through retirement comfortably. A lot depends on expenses, needs, and lifestyle. One person may do quite well on $500,000 during retirement, while another may burn through $5 million quickly. It's hard to believe, but according to a 2009 *Sports Illustrated* article, 78% of NFL players go bankrupt within five years of retirement.[12] As the saying goes, it's not what you make, it's what you keep that counts. A common mistake that do-it-yourselfers make is to assume the budget they're on today will suffice decades into the future. If you're living fine on $5,000 per month now, why not use that as your estimate? After all, expenses will go down, right?

While it's true some expenses may drop, others, such as health care expenses, will rise. One of the most overlooked increases in expenses comes from the newly found free time. When you're working, you spend five days a week in the office and two days a week on the golf course. When you're retired, you'll spend no time in the office—and every day on the golf course. Work weeks turn into weekends. Cooking at home turns into dining out. Days at the beach become getaways in

Tahiti. When your work time goes down, expenses go up. Not accounting for potential spending increases is a big reason why many end up being discouraged when they find out their nest egg isn't nearly large enough to fund their retirement lifestyle.

> Not accounting for potential spending increases is a big reason why many end up being discouraged when they find out their nest egg isn't nearly large enough to fund their retirement lifestyle.

Other calculations get a little fuzzy too. You may decide to sell your home to downsize, but what will home prices be at that time? How much will you owe in capital gains taxes? Perhaps you bought a smaller home, but there are now HOA dues you didn't have before. Maybe you need pool cleaning and yard service. There's no way to determine these costs because they're simply unknown.

The art side is more difficult—but critical—to your success. You need to have a good estimate of where you want to go. After all, you can't set your GPS if you don't know the address. Still, there are some guidelines to follow to help you figure out good estimates. Once you do, it's not too hard to work backward and figure out how much you should invest each month.

STEP #1: KNOW WHAT YOUR GOAL IS

Financial planners often use certain metrics to see if people are on track to retire by age sixty-five. Some say you should have 1.5 times your annual salary by age thirty-five, 4 times by age forty-five, and 7 times by age fifty-five.

Another method is to have enough saved to replace 75% of the salary from your most recent job before retiring. If you earned $100,000 in your last job, you should have a plan that can generate

$75,000 per year. As with all metrics, these must be used carefully, especially for people with extreme incomes, whether high or low. For instance, someone earning $25,000 per year will probably need much more than suggested by these measures when compared to a CEO making $20 million per year.

When planning for retirement, it's best to base your monthly expenses on dependable income streams, not your investments, because payments from Social Security, pensions, or annuities won't be affected by market fluctuations. If your monthly expenses can be met with certainty, you're more likely to allow your investment to grow—and compound—over time.

Retirement calculations are difficult because they're estimates. You must estimate future needs, rates of return, inflation, expenses, and emergency expenses, to name just a few. No matter which monthly figures you decide to use, it's a good idea to plan for more. Having too much money at retirement is a much better problem than not having enough. There are too many uncertainties in today's markets surrounding health care, housing, fuel costs, and even Social Security's solvency. It won't be surprising to see the government continue to increase the retirement age or decrease benefits.

However, that doesn't mean you should go overboard with estimates. Some people are tempted to intentionally overshoot their estimates to be sure they meet their goals. That's not a good solution. If you're investing far more money than you think is necessary, you're jeopardizing current needs and goals. It may mean the business you dreamed of building never gets off the ground, your kids don't go to college, and your insurance and emergency cash is underfunded. Overshooting the numbers to ensure a safe retirement may mean you're jeopardizing the very goal. Like all financial planning, balance is the key.

As an example, let's say you'll need $5,000 per month during retirement. Depending on how far off retirement is, you may need to account for the steady fall in the dollar's value—inflation—which ensures money won't go as far in the future. Let's say retirement is ten years away, and you're planning on 3% inflation. Your monthly needs are now increased to $5,000 × (1.03)10, or about $6,720. How will you come up with this money each month? This is where we work the problem backward.

STEP #2: HOW BIG IS YOUR STASH?

At this stage, add the values of all retirement accounts, including savings, 401(k) plans, IRAs, or other tax-advantaged accounts. Don't consider Social Security here, because those payments will be made in the future, and they can't be used to make up any shortfalls.

Next, you need to figure out if that amount can get you through retirement based on your monthly needs, and there are a couple easy ways to get estimates. First, financial planners often use the 4% rule, which says that if your money is invested in a well-diversified portfolio, you can withdraw 4% of the funds each year with an additional 3% each for inflation. At that rate, your money should last about thirty years.

Let's say you currently have saved $300,000 among all accounts. If you began withdrawing 4% today, you'd receive $12,000 the first year, or $1,000 per month. Each year after that, add 3% for inflation, so the second year you could withdraw $12,000 × (1.03), or $12,360. Next, add to this figure your estimated Social Security payments, which you can find at ssa.gov. Let's assume you expect to receive $1,000 per month from Social Security. Your expected monthly income now totals $2,000. However, you planned for $6,720, so you're short by $4,720. It's not a time to panic. Just time for a plan.

STEP #3: MAKE UP THE MISSING MONEY

Your current $300,000 savings must make up the shortfall, so continue to work backward. Your retirement funds must provide $6,720 per month less the $1,000 from Social Security, or $5,720. That means your future balance must be large enough so that a 4% annual withdrawal equals $5,720 × 12, or $68,640. In other words, your account's value must be $68,640 ÷ 0.04, or $1,716,000.

Let's check the math: If you have $1,716,000 and withdraw 4% per year, that's $68,640, or $5,720 per month. Add the $1,000 from Social Security, and there's your $6,720 target value. If you have $300,000 today but need just over $1.7 million, your money must increase nearly sixfold. It sounds like an impossible goal, but the power of compounding may take care of the bulk of the shortfall. You may not have the money, but you'll definitely need the discipline.

If you need $1.7 million and currently have $300,000, your money must grow by a factor of $1.7 million divided by $300,000, or 5.7 times. How long will that take?

It depends on the returns. There's a financial planning tool called the rule of 72, which shows how long it takes for money to double. Just divide 72 by the expected returns on your investments, and that's about how long it takes for your money to double. At 10% returns, it takes 72 ÷ 10, or 7.2 years to double. There's a related idea called the Rule of 114, which shows how long it takes for your money to triple. At 10%, it takes about 114 ÷ 10%, or 11.4 years to triple your money. In this example, you need about a sixfold increase on your money, which is the same as doubling it and then tripling it. So, if you add 7.2 years and 11.4 years, it'll take about 18.6 years to meet your goal. Don't worry about the calculations, as there's financial planning software that takes care of all that. The point is that it's straightforward math that allows you to make future projections.

Whenever you're making investment plans, remember that the long-term returns from the stock market vary depending on the time frame. Be conservative in your estimates. Don't hope for 20% per year just because that's what's required to accomplish your goals. It's not a realistic goal, and you're likely to end up taking more risk and end up taking losses. It's always better to set a realistic plan, even if it means you must work longer or contribute more money. It's better to have a working plan than a disappearing dream.

If we found that it would take nineteen years to accomplish your goal and your retirement is twenty years away, by doing nothing other than being patient, the magic of compounding will get you there. If retirement is twenty years away, by doing nothing other than being patient, the magic of compounding will get you to your goal. However, even if the calculations show that patience will do the trick, you should still plan to supplement your accounts with future deposits in case you don't achieve the expected investment rate of return.

What if you're behind? Unfortunately, most Americans are. When people discover they're behind, they decide to take more risk. Risk, however, is a double-edged sword, and while there's more room for gains—there's also more room for losses. The biggest problem with taking more risk, especially if you're within ten years of retirement, is that one big market drop—like during the COVID-19 pandemic—can destroy your goals. If you're planning to quit working soon, there's no money coming in, and a lot less to withdraw. There are safer ways to accomplish your goals without investing in penny stocks or dedicating a large portion of your salary to lottery tickets. If a safer route gets you to your goal, that's the better choice. Here are some places to start.

THE POWER OF ADDITIONAL CONTRIBUTIONS

If compounding and Social Security strategies don't allow you to meet retirement goals, you'll either have to work longer or make additional contributions. If you decide to invest more money, start small. The mistake most people make is to overcontribute and create a financial burden. They can't stay with the plan. It's far more important to make consistent, small deposits over longer time periods. Compounding does most of the work for you but only if you give it time.

Let's start with some easy choices with big advantages. If you participate in your employer's 401(k) or other tax-advantaged plan, be sure to contribute the full amount that qualifies for the company match. Matching dollars is usually part of a benefits package to attract talented employees.

The employer matches each dollar you contribute up to a certain limit. It may be a simple match, say up to $500 or $1,000. Other businesses may contribute a percentage, say 50% of the first 6% of your salary. A handful of the largest corporations will even match you dollar for dollar without limit. If you're lucky enough to work for such a company and behind on retirement savings, there's no other strategy to consider other than contributing the maximum to that plan first. Anytime someone guarantees 100% on your money, take it. No matter what type of plan your company offers, be sure to at least contribute enough to capture the full match. It's the easiest and safest 100% you'll ever make.

The maximum 2020 contribution to a 401(k) is $19,500 per year. While matching seems like an offer you can't refuse, many people do. There's no reason to not collect that money because they're part of your salary disguised as a benefit. It shouldn't matter to you if you earn $50,000 per year and $5,000 in 401(k) contributions, or $55,000 per year and no contributions. Companies create these perks to entice talented people, but employees who refuse to take the offer aren't just wasting time; they're wasting money. When it comes to investing, always take advantage of all guaranteed matches first.

ONE STEP AT A TIME

One of the key concepts for financial planning is to think incrementally—one step at a time. If you contribute an extra $1,000 per year and end up with almost $30,000 after fifteen years, it may seem like a lot of effort for little gain. That's the wrong way to look at it. Don't think about total dollars. Think incrementally. In the big picture, $30,000 isn't anything to get worked up over for fifteen years of work toward your retirement. But think about this: While you probably wouldn't jump at a job offer for $30,000 per year, you'd probably appreciate it if an additional $30,000 dropped into your lap right now. By itself, $30,000 isn't going to be a game changer, but you must look at how it will affect your overall financial picture. What if you owed that much on your house at retirement but could now pay it off? Those $2,000 monthly mortgage payments to your bank are now going in your pocket. That $30,000 just created an extra $2,000 per month. Even if you owed a lot more, say $100,000, paying down the mortgage by one-third may cut your payments in half. It all counts once you learn to think incrementally.

Even if it just allowed you to reduce your mortgage or other debt, lowering monthly bills may be the key that allows you to meet your retirement obligations. To contribute an extra $1,000 per year amounts to less than $85 per month. So even though those small contributions aren't going to fund your entire retirement, those small deposits, after compounding, will put you in a brighter future position.

Making IRA contributions may also provide tax benefits today. If you're using a traditional IRA, you'll reduce your current income by the amount of the contributions, which means you'll owe less in tax. You win today and tomorrow. If you're using a Roth IRA, you won't get any tax breaks today because you're contributing with after-tax dollars, but the benefit is you'll own no taxes upon withdrawal.

Also keep in mind that you're allowed to make the maximum contributions to your IRA, even if you're not qualified to get the tax deduction. For example, perhaps you or your spouse contribute to a 401(k) plan, and your modified adjusted gross income (MAGI) exceeds annual limits, so you may not be able to deduct the IRA contributions. However, that doesn't mean you can't make contributions. If you already have an IRA account set up, it's easy to contribute more money without opening another account. Also, consider opening a Roth IRA because, as we've discussed, those deposits must be made with after-tax dollars; the benefit is you won't pay any taxes upon withdrawal. Any gains made in either a traditional or Roth IRA will grow tax-free. That is, each time you sell a security, you won't owe capital gains taxes since the investing was done inside of an IRA. Even though you may not get today's tax deductions, it doesn't mean there's no point in contributing to an IRA. Growing the gains tax-free accelerates the compounding effect, so always maximize your IRA contributions first.

THE BREAKEVEN POINT—SOCIAL SECURITY

As with all financial decisions, there are many factors to consider, and receiving more money in the future doesn't necessarily mean you're better off. Remember, there are opportunity costs—a cost for waiting. If you take early retirement at age sixty-two, you'll take a lifetime reduction of up to 30%—but you'll also receive more checks.

The additional money could be used today to put you in a better financial position—and more than make up for the penalty.

For instance, it could be invested in the market. It could be used to pay off debt, which will put more money in your pocket today, save on interest, and also allow you to invest more into the market. So, is it better to get more checks with smaller amounts? Or fewer checks with larger amounts?

It turns out there's a mathematical point where there's no difference between the two choices, and that's called the *breakeven point*, which is simply the age at which both choices are the same. If you live longer than the breakeven point, it was beneficial to delay the checks. Otherwise, you'd be better off taking the penalty. It's not an easy calculation because there are many factors to consider such as the expected return you could make on your money, inflation, spousal benefits, and taxes, to name a few. The Social Security Administration has breakeven calculators on its website at ssa.gov that can help with individual decisions.

Some people will come out better by taking the penalty while others won't. The one thing that's certain is the longer you delay your checks, the higher the breakeven age becomes. That means you must live a lot longer before delaying becomes beneficial.

As a simple example, let's assume you'll receive $1,000 per month if you wait until full retirement age at sixty-six, but elect to take a 25% reduction and begin earning $750 at age sixty-two. That's an extra forty-eight months' worth of $750 checks, or $36,000 total that you would have missed by waiting.

By waiting until age sixty-six, you'll receive $1,000 rather than $750, for an extra $250 per month. To find the breakeven point, just answer a simple question: How many checks would you have to receive before the extra $250 per month equals the $36,000 you received over 4 years? That would take $36,000 ÷ $250 = 144 months, or twelve years. By delaying checks until age sixty-six, you'd need to live to age seventy-eight to make both decisions equal. If you live past seventy-eight, you'll be better off by delaying checks until age sixty-six. This is an oversimplified example so you can get the idea of the breakeven point. In practice, you'd have to account for money that could be earned by investing earlier, debts that could be paid off, inflation that will eat away at its value, and other factors.

If your family has a long history of not living past seventy-eight, it may be a better decision to take the money early, no matter how good the guaranteed extra 8% per year may seem. Even though it seems like a slam-dunk decision to delay benefits and collect an extra 8% per year, it's not quite that easy. Bigger checks come at the price of waiting, and the breakeven point provides insights into the decision.

IRMAA PREMIUM

Creative financial planning is about awareness—awareness of opportunities to have current laws work for you and not against you. It is vital you and your planner keep up with current laws and regulations. Medicare's income-related monthly adjustment amount, or IRMAA, is a premium charged by Medicare Parts B and D to those with higher incomes. For the first time in a decade, Medicare's premium surcharges will be indexed to inflation by using the consumer price index (CPI) as of January 2020. As a result, some may find a reduction in their Medicare surcharge costs.

Beginning January 1, the income-related monthly adjustment amount brackets used to determine high-income surcharges for individuals and married couples will be indexed to the consumer price index based on the 12-month CPI change from September 2018 through August 2019. The index showed an increase of 1.7% for August 2019, so the income brackets used to determine Medicare surcharges in 2020 will also increase by 1.7%, rounded to the nearest

$1,000. In response, income tiers will increase by $1,000 to $3,000 for individuals and $2,000 to $6,000 for those married filing jointly. Your 2020 Medicare surcharges will be based on your 2018 tax returns, so it's crucial to update your income information. Medicare generally uses your modified adjusted gross income (MAGI) from two years prior. Chances are, with COVID-19, your income is much less than two years ago, so simply updating your information can keep you from unnecessarily paying the additional premium.

ENJOY EARLY RETIREMENT WITH 72(T)

If you take early distributions from an IRA or other tax-advantaged accounts, such as a 401(k), you're generally subject to 10% early withdrawal penalties. That's steep. However, there are strategies that allow you to take early withdrawals but completely avoid the 10% penalties. One way is accomplished through a strategy called substantially equal periodic payments (SEPP), otherwise known as 72(t) distributions, and that can be a big boost toward an early retirement. You can begin taking distributions at any age. However, once you've started, you must continue for five years or until age 59½, whichever is longer. If you're 59 years old, for instance, you'd need to continue taking distributions until age 64. The IRS has three approved methods for calculating the amount of your distributions. First, you can take the required minimum distribution (RMD). Just take your account value on December 31 and divide it by your life expectancy according the one of three IRS tables.

Second, you can choose an amortization schedule, which is done by taking your account value on December 31 and dividing it by your life expectancy. This method creates identical revenue streams that'll never change. It will also usually create the highest payments. However, if you choose the RMD method, your payments will change according to IRS RMD calculations.

Third, you can elect an annuitization, which is similar to the second method, except that the IRS uses an annuity factor to determine the payments. This method produces income streams somewhere between the RMD and amortization methods.

Keep in mind, if you start a 72(t) and stop early or manage it incorrectly, you run the risk of owing a retroactive 10% penalty on all withdrawals you have taken. Make sure you know what you are doing and manage the plan well until you reach the five-year mark or age 59½ mark.

I urge you to not settle for a generic retirement plan. I have never met a client who was implementing every creative strategy that was available to them. Take the time to audit your plan and be willing to replace mediocre strategies with better ones. One of the best ways to get a financial reality check is to meet with an advisor who manages money for a living. There is a good chance that they have seen much more than you and have information you need. With that said, not all financial advisors are created equal, and you need to know what questions to ask before placing your financial future in their hands.

Chapter 11 Summary

1. **You need to have a goal in mind in order to set your retirement GPS.** Do you want to have $1M of liquid investments? Do you want to have $5,000 per month of retirement income? Once you have a goal in mind, you can work the math backward to determine what steps are necessary to achieve that goal. Don't just put your head down, work hard, and hope it works out.

2. **In our current society, the odds are heavily in your favor to live to an old age.** So don't live as if you are not going to need money later in life. Make decisions now that will make your future self proud—and secure.

3. **Social Security break-even point:** Do not underestimate the importance of this decision. Know the break-even point based on the day you decide to receive your payments.

4. **IRMMA Premium:** Many people overpay Medicare premiums without knowing it. If your income has dropped over the past two years, you do not want Medicare using your old income to decide your monthly premium. Provide them with accurate information.

CHAPTER 12

How to Work with a Financial Professional

Most people spend more time researching the next car or phone they will buy than the financial advisor they will work with.

Working with the right financial professional may open your eyes to new strategies and help you avoid big mistakes. Working with the wrong advisor can set your financial plan back years or decades and make you fearful of any future financial guidance. The stakes are high, and that is why I chose to include this chapter in the book.

FIDUCIARY VERSUS SUITABILITY STANDARDS

Imagine that you're sitting with a financial advisor who has selected a couple of mutual funds that are similar, and either would be suitable for your goals. One, however, charges a big up-front charge called a *sales load* while the other one doesn't, also called a *no-load* fund. Which should be recommended?

If you said the no-load fund, you might be right, but you might also be wrong. It depends on whether you're working with an advisor who operates by a *fiduciary* standard or one who operates by a *suitability* standard.

A fiduciary standard is the highest standard in the industry, and it requires the advisor to put the client's interests first. No actions may be taken that would benefit the advisor over the client. Most charge a fee for their advice or a percentage of assets they manage. For instance, if you have a $100,000 account being managed with a 1% AUM (assets under management) fee, it will cost $1,000 per year, or $83 per month, which is pretty cheap for unlimited, unbiased advice.

Naturally, as the account value rises or falls, so do the fees. This approach aligns the fiduciary's interests with yours because the advisor has a clear incentive to grow your account. Based on the description of a fiduciary, you'd think it would be the standard for the industry.

However, the majority of advisors fall under the *suitability* standard, which means they only have to be sure the products or advice are "suitable" for you, whether or not there are better or cheaper alternatives. They make these determinations based on your suitability profile you fill out when opening the account. As long as the financial product fits that goal, it doesn't matter if it's the best, the cheapest, or the least risky of the bunch. It only matters that it was suitable. There are great professionals in both groups, but the suitability standard leaves more room for interpretation of what is best for the client.

FOUR TYPES OF FIDUCIARIES

If that's not confusing enough, there are four different categories of fiduciary, and each has different rules to abide by.

1. One type of advisor works as a fiduciary under the SEC (Securities and Exchange Commission) as a registered investment advisor (RIA). These advisors are allowed to have outside affiliations with other broker-dealers and can receive commissions and referral fees, as long as they're disclosed.

2. A second type of advisor operates as a Department of Labor (DOL) fiduciary. These advisors are held to fiduciary standards but only for retirement advice. So, if they're giving advice about an IRA, they must act as a fiduciary, but if they're giving advice in a regular brokerage account, they don't have to act as a fiduciary. Strange, right?

3. The third type of fiduciary is the CFP (Certified Financial Planner), a designation I'm proud to hold. Candidates must pass rigorous exams and pledge to abide by the board's standards. The CFP standard is the broadest of all because it applies to all aspects of planning, not just retirement planning as with the DOL standard. On the downside, the CFP doesn't have a regulatory body, so clients can't sue for breach of fiduciary duties as they can under SEC and DOL, so you still want to be sure you interview people you're thinking of dealing with.

4. The fourth type of advisor doesn't operate under a single umbrella. Instead, these advisors sign voluntary pledges through many self-regulating organizations. For instance, the National Association of Personal Financial Planners (NAPFA) and XY Planning Network (XYPN) are two

common organizations. Another popular one is the Center for Fiduciary Excellence (CEFEX), which has the strictest standards because they require an annual audit of all advisors.

My team operates within an RIA, and I hold the CFP designation, so we take seriously the fiduciary obligation to our clients.

What does this mean for you?

If you are currently working with financial professionals, you should ask them if they are held to a fiduciary standard or a suitability standard. If it feels like they try to sidestep the question, I would encourage you to press for a straight answer. Remember, their answer does not tell you if they are a good advisor or not, it just lets you know what type of standard they are held to. It is then up to you to decide what you feel most comfortable with.

If you are looking for a new advisor, I would encourage you to add the fiduciary standard as a requirement.

WHY WORK WITH A FINANCIAL ADVISOR?

It should be clear that it's not easy to identify if an advisor truly has your best interests at heart. There are so many terms that can be confusing. So, the first big advantage of working with a trustworthy fiduciary advisor is that you'll have someone who can help you navigate through the difficult and sometimes murky world of financial products. The trouble is that many of these products are excellent and may be exactly what you're looking for. However, they could also be a disaster. Unless you're a financial professional and know where to look, it's easy to step into traps.

For instance, in 2007, many brokers were selling auction rate securities (ARS) as a substitute for cash—just with higher yields. Each week, banks would show up to bid and reset the interest rates. If it sounds confusing, don't worry: That's what brokers told clients too. The only thing that matters, they said, is that you'll earn more money than just leaving it as cash in your account. And hey, who doesn't want more money, right? It was an easy sale, and it worked great—until it didn't.

As the 2007–2008 financial crises unfolded, banks quit showing up for auctions, and once one auction failed, the entire thing collapsed. Investors couldn't get their cash back and instead were left holding illiquid investments with long-term maturities, which now left them vulnerable to interest rate risk. Nearly every brokerage firm received fines, but in December 2008, the SEC finalized settlements with Citigroup and UBS Securities for over $30 billion, which at the time were the largest settlements in SEC history. Assuming you even got your money back, what good did it do you if that money was intended to buy the perfect home at retirement, but you couldn't get your money out for over a year? Many brokers sold this investment option because their firm instructed them to. If your financial professional is incentivized to sell products you may also find yourself in a situation like this. Your advisor should have your best interest in mind at all times.

Here are some other benefits you get by working with a fiduciary advisor.

HELP MAKE SENSE OF COMPLEX DECISIONS

The financial world has always been complex, but with each passing year, the complexities grow. The earliest form of risk reduction dates back to 2000 BC, where Chinese and Babylonian merchants would distribute their goods among many ships to reduce the loss should one ship sink.

The earliest forms of insurance are recorded back to 300 BC, when sea merchants could take out insurance policies against their cargo, called a "bottomry," which gets its name because the collateral is effectively attached to the bottom of the ship. Merchants would borrow money to buy cargo, and if the ship arrived safely, the merchant returned the loan plus interest. But if the loan wasn't repaid, the lender would take possession of the ship and contents. Not only were sophisticated insurance products available, but so was fraud. A Greek merchant named Hegestratos took out a bottomry, sunk his ship, sold the contents, and kept the loan. However, his crew caught him in the act, and Hegestratos was thrown overboard and drowned.

Advance the clock to the twenty-first century, and insurance products have advanced to where few people understand them. For instance, we have credit default swaps (CDS) and synthetic collateralized debt obligations (CDO), both of which were partially responsible for the 2007–2008 financial crisis. As financial products advance, so do the complexities, and it's easy to buy a product that sounds right—until something goes wrong, as is made painfully obvious in the movie *The Big Short*. If JP Morgan and other big-name firms can get on the wrong side, it's not hard for retail investors to make the same poor choices. The people selling these products are highly trained to tell you just enough to pass the legalities, but most investors cannot explain the small print if asked.

EXPERIENCE

Another benefit is experience. You want to work with an advisor who's been through market cycles, earnings cycles, sector rotations, bubbles, and crashes. If market prices are skyrocketing, it's easy to get caught up in the euphoria and want to take out a second mortgage to buy more shares. It's a near guarantee you'll end up with an overweight portfolio, and you'll pay a big price once prices retreat.

On the other hand, when markets crash, it's easy to panic and sell your investments. Most people do. I've heard people justify it by saying they'll get back into the market once the time is right, but at least they'll stop the losses for now. Well, I always wonder, if they were so good at getting in when the time is right, why didn't they do it before? Why were they just caught selling at a loss?

Everyone thinks they can get in and out of the market when the time is right. If it were only that easy. It sounds like a good idea, but you'll end up buying high and selling low, hardly a recipe for success.

A good financial advisor will help you to keep the proper perspective, will explain what's happening in the market, and will guide you through the right steps to make the best of it. That person is like a sports coach who reminds a player to stick with the plan of attack that was agreed upon before a match. If left to their own decisions, players who are losing halfway through a match will want to switch strategies. It sounds like a good idea if they're losing,

> When market prices are flying high, use the opportunity to sell into the strength, a tactic that's called *fading the market*.

but it usually means they'll lose in a different way—and faster. The better approach to investing is to react to the market, not predict it. When market prices fall, use the opportunity to buy shares at fire-sale prices. It'll pay off in the future. When market prices are flying high, use the opportunity to sell into the strength, a tactic that's called *fading the market*. That too is easier said than done, and that's where a great financial advisor will be worth their weight in gold.

Experience doesn't just help with the emotional side of investing. Every year, laws change, tax brackets change, exchange rates change, and market prices change. The market is in a constant state of change, and that means you must be too. But how?

Should you contribute more money to an IRA? Should it be a traditional or Roth? Will tariffs help or harm your investments? What will they do to exchange rates? Should you use A, B, or C shares for mutual funds? The list of questions goes on and on, and each correct decision can put you closer to your financial goals. It's not worth guessing. There's a ton of information on the internet, but how will you weed through it all? And, more important, which sites can you trust?

TAX PLANNING

Tax planning is another area where financial planners can improve your plan. Will a purchase or sale be in violation of the wash-sale rule? How should you alter your choices? What are the advantages of tax deferrals? Should you shift from short-term to long-term? How can you shift to lower tax brackets? Will it be beneficial to harvest tax losses?

Can you save 12% in taxes by using 1256 contracts? How can ETFs make your investments more tax efficient because of their redemption process? Entire books have been written on the business of tax planning, but it's just one small part of your financial picture. Most people will not spend the time needed to research these questions, so they settle for paying more taxes than they should and making mistakes that they will later regret.

ADVISOR ALPHA STUDY—CAN AN ADVISOR ADD SIGNIFICANT VALUE?

While I have seen over and over the value that a good advisor can add to a client's financial plan, it always helps to get data from a third party to validate that stance. Vanguard is one of the largest investment firms in the country and is well known for its low-cost mutual funds and ETFs. In the past, Vanguard has been seen as a competitor to advisors who make compensation from commissions on mutual funds sales.

While that may be true, firms like mine use Vanguard funds if they are best for our clients and see them as a partner instead of a competitor.

In 2001, Vanguard produced a study known as the Advisor Alpha.[13] The purpose of this study was to calculate the various ways advisors can add value for their clients and arrive at a measurable benefit. The study, which has been continuously updated, provides valuable insight. The 2019 study found the following benefits:

SUITABLE ASSET ALLOCATION

Benefit—valuable but too many variables to quantify

Explanation: Understanding the client's goals and risk tolerance to assist in purchasing the right mix of investments such as stocks, bonds, and cash. Important to avoid "investment overlap," which we discussed earlier in the book. Many people think they are diversified when in fact they are not.

COST-EFFECTIVE IMPLEMENTATION

Benefit—45 basis points (or 0.45%)

Explanation: Knowing how to buy the right investments at the lowest available cost. The same investment can be packaged in multiple ways with varying fee structures. The value could be even larger if compared to higher-cost funds. It can be very frustrating as a client to know you are holding a more expensive version of an investment just because you or your current advisor doesn't know about this strategy.

REBALANCING

Benefit—35 basis points (or 0.35%)

Explanation: Based on performance of different investments within your accounts, the allocation you originally set will begin to change. If you believe a 60% stock, 40% bond balance is best for you, it is important to periodically rebalance to that allocation. If stocks have a great year, they may end up becoming 80% of your account. Active rebalancing allows you to sell investments while they are high and buy lower-performing investments at a discount to return to your desired allocation. Part of the science of this strategy is not overusing it.

BEHAVIORAL COACHING

Benefit—150 basis points (or 1.5%)

Explanation: Providing discipline and guidance can be the largest potential value-add available to advisors. Helping our clients avoid making decisions based on news headlines or extreme emotion is a big part of my job. While I do believe strategies should change when necessary, clients need to believe in their plan and stick to it to have success.

ASSET LOCATION

Benefit—0 to 75 basis points (or 0.75%)

Explanation: We discussed earlier that the type of investment you buy is not the only consideration. You need to know what type of account to hold the investment within. A high-growth, long-term investment would thrive in a Roth IRA where it receives tax-free treatment. However, you would not want to own a tax-free municipal bond within a Roth IRA because the tax-free treatment of the bond would be less impactful.

SPENDING STRATEGY (WITHDRAWAL ORDER)

Benefit—0 to 70 basis points (or .70%)

Explanation: We help our clients build investments within

three buckets: tax-free, tax-deferred, and taxable. Each bucket receives different tax treatment and can be more or less beneficial depending on the current tax laws when the funds are withdrawn. For example, if clients have earned income and tax rates are high, we may decide to withdraw funds from their Roth IRA. Or, if clients' tax rates are low in a given year, we may decide to take income from their traditional IRA and taxable investment account.

TOTAL-RETURN VERSUS INCOME INVESTING

Benefit—valuable but too many variables to quantify

Explanation: Longstanding strategies related to creating income from investments may not hold up very well as a result of interest rate fluctuations and market performance. I wish it were as simple as investing in a diversified portfolio and just living off dividends and interest. The income alone generated from many portfolios today will not satisfy clients' needs during retirement. Knowing what investments to own and what risks are associated with those investments can be the difference between having enough income during retirement or having to reduce your lifestyle. Or worse, be forced to go back to work.

As you can see, this was a detailed report from Vanguard, and it provides valuable insight. The result of the study was that capable advisors can add around *3% of value per year* to their clients. Take some time and evaluate the value your advisor is providing to make sure you are not missing out. Not every advisor is capable of advising to this extent, so you need to ask good questions and be honest with yourself if you need to make a change.

In today's online world, there's no shortage of "fintech" websites or phone apps that will manage money for you. The problem is that people are trying to design software that uses "one size fits all" investing. It's like trying to design a shoe that fits everyone, so it ends up fitting no one. Fintech planning software is probably okay for someone who just wants to set up a basic savings plan to put money away or make periodic investments into the stock market.

At the end of this book, you'll find Bonus Strategies that will elevate your financial plan even further.

I hope I've been able to help you focus on your financial picture in a new way, and I also hope you're hungry to learn more.

If you have thought "*I wish I knew that sooner*" to yourself even one time, reach out to my team and give us a shot to impress you. Our company does not require clients to transfer money to us to manage or fire their current advisors. Clients pay us to step in and give them a second look. Sometimes, that means a complete overhaul of a plan, or it may result in a few adjustments that lower your fees, reduce your tax bill, and increase your confidence that you are on the right track.

Chapter 12 Summary

1. **The right advice can be worth the advisor's weight in gold.** The wrong advice could set your financial plan back years, or worse, cause you to avoid financial advice in the future. Don't settle for generic, convenient financial advice. In today's world, you can access an advisor anywhere in the country, so work with the best you can.

2. **Fiduciary versus suitability**: A fiduciary must act in your best interest while a non-fiduciary has to provide suitable advice. Which one sounds better to you?

3. **The risk of making a mistake by not knowing what you don't know is very high for most people.** Be open to receiving professional feedback before you make major financial decisions.

4. **Advisor Alpha study**: Would you pay $100 if it generated $300? Read about this study to understand the various ways a good advisor can add value to your financial plan. Free advice does not tend to be the best advice.

Work with Our Team

Reach out to my team to learn how our strategies can improve your financial plan. Don't risk wishing you would have known sooner. Time is something that you can't get back.

InvestLegacy.com

Wish I Knew That Sooner Bonus Strategies

1) BACKDOOR ROTH IRA

Great strategy to build tax-free retirement, but make sure it is filed appropriately with the IRS. My team runs into many situations where either the CPA was not notified by the advisor of the strategy or someone filing their own taxes doesn't know how to report it.

2) ROTH 401(K)

Funding Roth IRAs can be limited based on your income, but Roth 401(k) accounts do not have income limits, and they have much higher contribution limits.

3) SEP IRA VERSUS SOLO 401(K)

SEP IRA contribution limits are a percentage of your income, so you may not be able to contribute as much as you want. However, solo 401(k) plans limit your contributions to a dollar amount, not a percentage. You may be able to contribute a lot more to a solo 401(k) than you can to a SEP IRA.

4) DEDUCTING FINANCIAL ADVICE

Many advisors receive their compensation through commissions or other fees charged from the sale of products or fees within a client's investment account. However, if you own a business, and the advisor is providing any services that benefit your business, they should charge you a flat fee for that time. That portion of your fee would then be tax deductible to your business. They would need to adjust the investment-management fee they are charging you to a lower level because they are now charging you directly for part of their services.

5) TAX HARVESTING

I routinely review financial plans that lack creative tax strategies. If you had nonretirement investments during the 2008 crash or the 2020 COVID crisis, you should have been harvesting losses when the market fell. If you held a position from the top to the bottom and back to the top again, you received very little benefit for your emotional roller coaster ride. My firm proactively sold investments at the bottom and replaced them with different investments. This allowed our clients to write off the losses on taxes for 2020, and then, because they still own other investments, they get to participate in the recovery. Bank the losses to use as you see fit. You may sell an investment property or other asset with a large gain, and now you have banked losses to reduce or negate your tax burden.

6) ESTATE TRUST PLANNING

Consider not placing firm ages on when money is forced upon your beneficiaries. It was standard for years to give beneficiaries some money when they turned thirty and more at thirty-five and more at forty, or some other sequence of ages to spread out the money. You have no idea what will be going on in the lives of your heirs, and you don't want to force money onto them if they don't want it. You can use language that gives them more access to funds at different ages but leave them the option to keep the funds in the trust if they want to.

7) MUTUAL FUNDS IN NONRETIREMENT ACCOUNTS

Tax efficiency of positions within a Roth IRA or traditional IRA is not as vital because gains are not recognized from year to year. You report the amount of distributions, not earnings. Nonqualified or nonretirement investment accounts are treated on a short-term or long-term capital-gain basis, and therefore, you recognize taxes each year to some extent. Mutual funds are managed toward a specific goal, and they don't care if you are a college freshman buying your first mutual fund and are in essentially a 0% tax bracket, or if you are a business owner in the highest tax bracket; the fund will be managed the same. The downside is that the fund will buy and sell investments all along, creating unnecessary taxes for the owner. Many financial firms have generic investment models that are very tax inefficient. I have seen clients with other advisors lose a lot of money in their portfolios and still have to pay taxes at the end of the year. That is a tough pill to swallow. Make sure you are evaluating tax efficiency of your investments.

8) IRA WITHDRAWALS BEFORE MANDATORY AGE

You may not need funds from your IRA account until age seventy-two, at which point they will be forced upon you under current tax law. That being said, you don't know what tax rates will be in the future, and it could be in your best interest to fill up your tax bracket each year before you get to that point.

For example, let's say you are currently paying 12% effective tax, and you would be allowed to earn $15,000 more this year before you jump to the next bracket. Even if you are sixty-two years old and not required to withdraw funds, you could take out $15,000 from your IRA and move it into another account to keep your taxes on those dollars. You can continue this each year to reduce the value of your IRA before you turn seventy-two and get as much money out of the IRA at the lowest tax rate possible.

9) QUALIFIED OPPORTUNITY ZONES

This tax law is being held out as one of the greatest tax-planning vehicles in history. If utilized appropriately, an investor could shelter a significant amount of capital gains and pay 0% capital gains after ten years. Investors need to be aware of Qualified Opportunity Funds, and real estate investors need to know how to participate in this strategy.

10) LONG-TERM CARE HYBRID LIFE INSURANCE

Many investors have some form of life insurance and believe they need it for a period of time. In addition, people worry about long-term care expenses later in their life but often can't bring themselves to add the additional expense for the fear they will never use it or concern that the price will keep going up. Consider adding long-term-care benefits to a life insurance policy so the dollars you are allocating can serve a dual purpose. You don't know if you will need long-term-care insurance, but I can promise you will cash in on your life insurance someday. We all will! If you never need long-term care, then you still have your life insurance policy, and if you end up needing long-term care, you can access some or most of your death benefit to cover those expenses.

11) TAX CREDITS

If your business has spent time and money on the improvement or development of a product in the past or present, or it will in the future, you need to be aware of available tax credits. We have helped small, medium, and large businesses find millions of dollars of tax credits that they did not know existed. Unfortunately, many CPAs do not have the expertise in this space; therefore, their clients do not reap the benefits. Consider finding a CPA firm that is knowledgeable in this space and ask for a high-level scope. You don't want to pay for it until you know it will be worth your time.

12) ASSET LOCATION

You have probably heard about "asset allocation," but you might not have heard about "asset location." Think of asset allocation helping you get the proper returns for the risk taken and asset location as efficient tax strategy. When building your portfolio, it is important that you consider the characteristics of each asset type (stocks, taxable bonds, municipal bonds, mutual funds, ETFs, REITs) and the account type (traditional IRAs, taxable, Roth, trusts) before investing. You might not want to invest in municipal bonds in an IRA or high-turnover mutual funds in your taxable joint account.

13) TAX LOT MANAGEMENT

Inside your nonqualified accounts, you want to take advantage of selling selectively. If you are reducing your position in a stock or harvesting capital losses, be careful to trade the proper lots. Every time you purchase more shares (including capital gains and dividend reinvestments), you now have a new lot for tax purposes. If you sell just five shares, the trading platform will assume certain lots for you, and it might not be the smartest tax decision.

14) RULE OF 55

Everyone knows that you cannot distribute from your retirement account until after age 59½, but that isn't technically true. If you leave an employer in the year of your fifty-fifth birthday or any age after, you can access your 401(k)/403(b) assets without paying the IRS's 10% penalty. So if you are retiring early or get laid off and need to access retirement funds, you have the option. This benefit is not available if you rollover funds into an IRA or try to access an old employer retirement account. Therefore, you should consolidate your old 401(k) plans into your current plan.

15) RULE 72(T)

Here is another loophole to the IRS's 10% early withdrawal penalty before age 59½. This rule allows you to take distributions from your IRA with special stipulations. You must make at least five substantially equal periodic payments annually of an amount calculated by IRS life-expectancy methods. It is important to distribute the exact amount to avoid penalties.

16) HSA USAGE AT SIXTY-FIVE

Before age sixty-five, health savings account assets used for anything except qualified medical expenses will be subject to a 20% penalty and will be included in your annual taxable income. Ouch! However, do not worry about overfunding this account, because after age sixty-five, distributions can be made for anything without the penalty. If you do not use it on qualified medical expenses, you will simply include the distributed amount in your annual income, and you enjoyed the tax-deferred growth on those assets.

17) INVEST YOUR HSA ASSETS

Another reason why an HSA is such a great savings vehicle is that you can actually invest your assets. This means that annual contributions and growth can help you cover the expected and unexpected health care costs now and in retirement. Be aware that investing involves risk and fees, so carefully consider your risk tolerance and time horizon before trading. Also, some trading platforms have minimum funding requirements or limited investment options, so again, research your available options.

18) FILL UP TAX BRACKETS

Remember that the federal income tax brackets are not a cliff schedule. This means that every dollar of income is first taxed at the lowest rate and then at subsequent rates until all income is accounted for. Thus, it is tax efficient to utilize all available space within the bracket you are currently in without pushing more income into the next. This is particularly important in retirement when your income is largely dependent on tax-deferred account distributions and Social Security. Therefore, strategize with your advisor to make distributions in your low-income years to "fill up your tax brackets," so that distributions in the future will not be taxed at higher rates.

19) DONOR-ADVISED FUNDS

If giving to charity is important to you, then you need to know about donor-advised funds. These accounts allow you to make a tax-deductible contribution, grow it tax deferred (if invested), and then give it tax-free to a charitable organization of your choice. This helps consolidate your tax-deductible gifts under one account and even prefund gifts for future years. There are fees and risk involved again if you invest, so be sure to evaluate your options before trading.

20) SELL YOUR HOME AND PAY NO TAXES

Did you know you could sell your home and pay no taxes on the gains? The IRS allows individuals to exclude $250,000 ($500,000 for married couples) in gains on the sale of your primary residence. There is a stipulation that you must know. You had to have lived there for two out of the past five years to be eligible. Remember that any improvements (not repairs) you make to the home can add to your cost basis and reduce your capital gains, so keep good records of expenditures.

21) REVERSE GIFT

When you gift assets to someone, they will most often assume your adjusted basis. Therefore, the asset with its gains is included in their estate. A reverse gift is when you gift assets to someone who will likely predecease you, and then, they leave the gifted asset back to you. This means you inherit the asset with a stepped-up basis as of the date of death. To be eligible, the gift must have been completed at least one year before the other person's death.

22) GIFTING OVER ALLOWED ANNUAL LIMIT

In 2020, you can gift up to $15,000 to anyone without paying gift tax. This amount covers most, but some people want to give even more than that. So if you gift more than the annual exclusion amount, don't worry. The IRS gives each person a lifetime gift tax exclusion amount that you can dip into, which for 2020, is $11.58 million. Any amount over this exclusion is subject to gift tax, and the rates do increase steeply. Even if you do not owe any gift taxes, you should still file a gift tax return to document use of your lifetime gift tax exclusion credit.

23) LIFE INSURANCE CONVERSION OPTIONS

Most people would prefer to have a term life insurance policy that, if needed, has the ability to turn into another policy in the future. You can turn a term policy into a permanent policy or even add long-term care benefits if you set it up correctly on the front end. This feature may add a few dollars per month to the cost on the front end but could be well worth it down the road.

24) GIFT DIRECTLY FROM IRA ACCOUNTS

If you gift directly from IRAs to 501(c)(3), it will not show as taxable income to you. Even though you get a deduction when you gift the funds, if it flows through your bank account first, it could increase your AGI and therefore your effective tax rate.

25) YOU DO NOT HAVE TO REINVEST DIVIDENDS

When you purchase stocks or mutual funds, you can choose to have income paid to your account in cash. There are reasons for doing this. You may want to the cash for income, or you may not want to buy more of that investment automatically. Maybe the price is really high, and you want to accumulate the cash to buy at a later date. Automatically reinvesting dividends can be a great idea to buy more shares but, depending on your situation, it may not always be the best default.

26) BASIS STEP UP AT DEATH

Your basis—that is, the amount of a given investment you have already paid tax on, automatically steps up at your death. This is important because you may plan to gift an asset while living that you should in fact hold and gift upon your passing. For example, let's assume you paid $500 for a stock, and it appreciated to $1,000. If you gift that asset while you're living, you also gift your basis of $500, so the recipient would have to pay tax on $500 of growth when they sell it. However, if you leave the $1,000 asset upon your death, the beneficiary will receive a step up in basis to $1,000 and will not have a taxable gain. Be strategic about types of investments and when you gift them.

27) BE WARY OF INVESTING A LARGE AMOUNT ON ONE DAY

Consider spreading your investment over a period of days, weeks, or months. A negative return early in your investment can impact long-term returns dramatically. In 2020, a client of mine sold a business and had a large amount of cash available. We developed a plan to invest the funds over a period of six months or as opportunity presented. The following months were the peak of the COVID-19 crisis, and the market crashed. Since we did not invest all the funds right away, we had a lot of cash to buy in after the market drop. This strategy saved the client over one million dollars in losses and then resulted in substantial gains.

28) PAID TO BE IN THE GAME

Even if the market is flat, you are most likely still making money. Many investments pay capital gains and dividends. For example, if you own a fund that pays a dividend and/or capital gains, you don't need the stock price to go up to earn money. However, you do need to stay invested. If you move to cash, you may miss your chance at capturing the dividend/capital-gain payouts.

29) TAX ARBITRAGE IN RETIREMENT

No one knows where tax rates will be when you retire. So in order to reduce your long-term tax risk while also avoiding taxes in the short term, we take a diversified approach. Consider investing in tax-deferred, tax-free, and taxable investments. These three types of accounts are all taxed differently, so when you get to retirement, you can withdraw just enough from each to control your tax bracket. If you have only tax-deferred investments, all of your withdrawals will be taxed, and you are at the mercy of tax rates.

30) REFINANCING AT A LOWER RATE MAY NOT ALWAYS BE BETTER

Most mortgages are structured to be heavy interest and less principal in the early years. If you constantly refinance, you can get stuck in a cycle of paying mostly interest, even if your rate is slightly lower. You then need to consider any closing costs and fees that apply to the refinance that may put you farther behind.

31) AUTOMATE YOUR INVESTING STRATEGY

Consider automating as much of your financial plan as possible. This will remove most of the excuses we all have for not getting around to it. For example, set up contributions to your retirement and investment accounts to come out automatically from your bank. You can always add more if necessary but have some amount transfer automatically. You may also select for your 401(k) or 403(b) contribution to automatically increase by 1% per year. We have found that most people intend to do the smart thing such as invest consistently or pay down debt more quickly, but life gets in their way. Something else comes up, and time flies by. Time is one of your great assets, so don't let it work against you.

32) IGNORING YOUR 401(K) INVESTMENTS

Make sure you review your 401(k) investments periodically. You need to know if there are lower cost options that have similar investments as higher priced funds you may own. You also need to evaluate if the funds you own have overlap that makes you less diversified than you think. I recommend that you review your 401(k) investments at least once each year. When you do, you can also consider rebalancing your account to make sure you are not overweight in an investment that happened to have a really good year. History has shown that the best performing asset class can quickly become one of the worst. If that happens to you, you'll wish you had sold while it was high. Rebalancing can help you avoid that regret.

33) ACTIVE REBALANCING

Timing the best day to buy and best day to sell in the market is a losing game over time. You may hit a good run a few times, but the market tends to catch up with you and take back those gains. However, I do not believe you should buy investments and set them on a shelf to gather dust. My team uses active rebalancing to force us to sell positions while they are high and buy other positions when they are low.

34) PENSION—TO TAKE LUMP SUM OR NOT?

The answer is that it depends. It depends on your risk tolerance and what the company is offering. If you take the monthly payment from the company, that decision takes the work to manage the funds off your plate, but you also run the risk of passing away and not realizing the full benefit you earned. Unfortunately, I have seen companies that offered a lump sum that was nowhere near the value of the monthly payment option. Don't be distracted by the big lump-sum number and jump to a decision. Use the 4% rule to determine how much income you can create with the lump sum. Here's an example: If the company is offering you $1,000 per month from the pension or $150,000 lump sum, what should you do? By applying the 4% rule, we get $150,000 * 4% = $6,000 per year, or $500 per month. In this scenario, it would be hard to choose the lump sum unless you were confident you would not live long enough to take enough income and you wanted your beneficiaries to receive some benefit.

35) COMPLICATED IS NOT ALWAYS BETTER

In my experience, the best financial plan is one that my client understands and will stick with. Do not fall in the trap of believing the best financial strategies are those that sound complicated and that most people will not understand. I have met clients who funded "boring" investments for thirty years without a hiccup and ended up in a better place than a client who chased every exciting new idea. Creative strategies will accelerate your success, but there are many paths to financial independence.

36) DON'T LET YOUR PAST EXPERIENCE WITH AN INVESTMENT CREATE UNREASONABLE LOYALTY OR DISLOYALTY TO AN INVESTMENT

As we discussed earlier, emotions are not your friend when it comes to financial planning and investing. You need to make wise decisions in the moment and try your best not to let past experiences or future hopes drive you. Just because you sell an investment does not mean you think it is bad. It may be a good time to sell it for tax purposes, or perhaps it has reached an all-time high, and you want to take some earnings off the table. Nothing will stop you from buying more back in the future if it is a good decision. Loyalty with investments only flows one way. If the stock drops dramatically, you will not receive a loyal customer refund in the mail.

Acknowledgments

Without a great team, my company would not be what it is today, and this book would not have been written. Thank you, Legacy Team.

Bill Johnson, this project started in a Panera Bread. It was a pleasure working with you.

Bonnie Hearn Hill, your positive energy and writing skills took us over the finish line. Thank you for showing such care and attention.

Endnotes

1   Deborah Thorne et al., "Graying of U.S. Bankruptcy: Fallout from Life in a Risk Society," *Indiana Legal Studies Research Paper* 406 (November 2018).

2   Marie Haaland, "Americans spend at least $18,000 a year on these nonessential costs," *SWNS Digital* (May 2, 2019).

3   Chris Hydock, Sezer Ulku, and Shiliang Cui, "Making the Wait Worthwhile: Mental Accounting and the Effect of Waiting in Line on Consumption," *Advances in Consumer Research* 46 (2018).

4   "NASDAQ 100, Historical Data," Yahoo Finance, accessed January 3, 2021, https://finance.yahoo.com/quote/%5ENDX/history/.

5   "Famous Cases and Criminals: ENRON," FBI, accessed January 13, 2021, https://www.fbi.gov/history/famous-cases/enron.

6   "Microsoft Corporation (MSFT)," Yahoo Finance, chart, accessed January 13, 2021, https://finance.yahoo.com/quote/MSFT/chart.

7   "Facebook, Inc. (FB)," Yahoo Finance, chart, accessed January 13, 2021, https://finance.yahoo.com/quote/FB/chart.

8   "S&P 500 (^GSPC," Yahoo Finance, chart, accessed January 13, 2021, https://finance.yahoo.com/quote/FB/chart.

9   "The Home Depot, Inc. (HD)," Yahoo Finance, chart, accessed January 13, 2021, https://finance.yahoo.com/quote/HD/chart.

10   "SPDR S&P 500 ETF Trust (SPY), Historical Data," Yahoo Finance, accessed January 13, 2021, https://finance.yahoo.com/quote/SPY/history.

11   Jane Gravelle, "Capital Gains Tax Options: Behavioral Responses and Revenues," Congressional Research Service, May 2020.

12   Lee Steinberg, "5 Reasons Why 80% Of Retired NFL Players Go Broke," *Forbes.com*, February 9, 2015.

13   Francis M. Kinniry, Jr., CFA, et. al. "Putting a value on your value: Quantifying Vanguard Advisor's Alpha," Vanguard, whitepaper, February 2019, https://advisors.vanguard.com/iwe/pdf/ISGQVAA.pdf.

Printed in the USA
CPSIA information can be obtained
at www.ICGtesting.com
JSHW012027140824
68134JS00033B/2913